AIR FRYER INSTANT POT Cookbook

100 Recipes to Cook
with Your Air Fryer & Instant Pot Pressure Cooker

Sara Quessenberry
Kate Merker
Anna Helm Baxter

CHARTWELL
BOOKS

Brimming with creative inspiration, how-to projects, and useful information to enrich your everyday life, Quarto Knows is a favorite destination for those pursuing their interests and passions. Visit our site and dig deeper with our books into your area of interest: Quarto Creates, Quarto Cooks, Quarto Homes, Quarto Lives, Quarto Drives, Quarto Explores, Quarto Gifts, or Quarto Kids.

ISBN 978-0-7858-3866-1

10 9 8 7 6 5 4 3 2 1

Library of Congress Control Number: 2020938492

Text and Recipes: Sara Quessenberry, Kate Merker, and Anna Helm Baxter
Publisher: Rage Kindelsperger
Editorial Director: Jeannine Dillon
Creative Director: Laura Drew
Managing Editor: Cara Donaldson
Senior Editor: Erin Canning
Project Editor: Leeann Moreau
Art Director: Merideth Harte
Cover Design: Cindy Laun
Interior Design: 3&Co. and Rebecca Pagel
Food Stylist: Sara Quessenberry
Assistant Food Stylist: Monica Pierini
Photography: Evi Abeler with the exception of cover and
    pages 13, 24, 43, 56, 76, 89, 102, 114, 119, 135, and 153 from Shutterstock

Printed in Singapore

Contents

INTRODUCTION

So you finally got an Instant Pot... congratulations!

Perhaps you've read all the incredible reviews from bloggers, chefs, and home cooks and decided to get an Instant Pot. Or maybe you have a friend who WON'T stop raving about it, and you caved and bought one of your own. Possibly, you received one as a gift.

Well, no matter how you got your Instant Pot, you must now be wondering what you're supposed to do with this magical appliance. You've heard it can cook eggs, meat, pasta, rice, vegetables, cheesecake, and more, but you have no idea how to get started. Don't worry—you're not alone! We are here to help. First off, we want to reassure you—the rumors are all true.

In case you weren't sure, this is definitely not your grandmother's stovetop pressure cooker. It doesn't squeal. And it certainly won't explode. In fact, the Instant Pot is an electric pressure cooker, and it is capable of so much more than those single-function pots from days of yore. Not only does it pressure-cook your food, often cutting cooking time at least by half (think dried beans in 45 minutes without soaking), it also has a built-in slow cooker for those days when you want dinner ready the moment you walk in the door after a long day.

So what's the difference between a pressure cooker and a slow cooker? With a pressure cooker, steam builds pressure, raising the boiling point, so food cooks faster. Translation: You can have stew on a school night and still have time to do homework.

A slow cooker, on the other hand, uses low temperatures and a lot of time to cook a meal. In other words: Throw ingredients in and forget it. With the Instant Pot, you get the best of both worlds. You don't just save time, you add diversity to meal planning and simplify your life in the kitchen by getting everything in a single appliance. No more cluttered countertops—HUGE bonus for anyone living in an apartment or home with a small kitchen!

"You can make stew on a school night and still have time to do homework!"

The many functions of the Instant Pot provide a versatility that you could never achieve with just a slow cooker or pressure cooker alone. Take the sauté mode (one of our favorites): Yes, it does the obvious, and sautés onions and garlic to bring out their true flavors; but it also sears meat to lock in flavor and form that desirable golden-brown crust; and it simmers sauces, so you can reduce them down to the perfect consistency.

This book has all the recipes you need to get started using your Instant Pot, including old-fashioned favorites, such as Pulled Pork Sandwiches (page 94) and Potato Salad with Mustard Vinaigrette (page 46). It will also give you the inspiration to stretch and experiment with delicious new flavors in dishes like Braised Lamb Souvlaki (page 65) and Pozole soup (page 99). We also give you a breakdown on what you absolutely need to know about the Instant Pot, including what the buttons do (page 8) and what rookie mistakes to avoid (pages 9 and 12). We use everyday ingredients in the recipes, nothing exotic or difficult to find.

Throughout the book, there are two types of "button" icons at the top of each recipe. The icons below indicate whether the recipe is meant for Air Fryer or Instant Pot.

The second set of "buttons" icons indicate which function you will use on your Instant Pot to cook the recipe. In the case of a few slow-cook recipes, we also provide an alternative pressure-cooked version of the recipe on the same page (just in case you don't want to wait 8 hours). Below are the button icons you'll see throughout the book, and you will find the corresponding buttons on your Instant Pot for when you start cooking.

Hopefully, you will take comfort and pride in making these recipes and gain the know-how and inspiration to create new recipes of your own. Before you know it, you'll want to cut back on take-out and fast foods, and get back to making quick and easy dinners every night at home. The Instant Pot can handle the pressure so you don't have to!

What you absolutely need to know before using your instant pot.

We know some of you want to dive right in and get started using your Instant Pot, so in this section, we have compiled the essential things you need to know to get started: how to release the steam when pressure cooking, the function of the buttons on the digital display, and the most common mistakes that rookies make—fortunately, we made them so you don't have to!

THE BUTTONS

> To change the time for any function, use the **+** or **−** keys to increase or decrease the desired time.

> The [**ADJUST**] button changes the slow cook temperature from "less" to "normal" to "more." It will also adjust the sauté temperature.

> Use the [**PRESSURE**] button to change the pressure setting between "low pressure" and "high pressure."

> When using the [**MANUAL**] setting, adjust to cook on low or high pressure by pressing the [**PRESSURE**] button. Then use **+** or **−** to set the time.

> To sauté, press the [**SAUTÉ**] button. It is automatically set to "Normal," which is what we used for all of our recipes. But if you would like less heat or more heat, press the [**ADJUST**] button to change between "Less," "Normal," or "More." When the temperature has been reached, the display will show "Hot." This is for open-lid cooking only.

> When slow cooking, press the [**SLOW COOK**] button and then the [**ADJUST**] button to select "Less," "Normal," or "More." Then use the **+** or **−** to adjust the time. For all of our slow-cooker dinners, we used the "More" setting for 8 hours.

> To steam, press the [**STEAM**] button and then the [**PRESSURE**] button to adjust for low or high pressure. Then use the **+** or **−** to adjust the time.

> When using the Soup, Meat/Stew, Bean/Chili, or Poultry settings, each one has a specified pressure and amount of time. You can change them to high or low pressure by pressing the [**PRESSURE**] button, and you can change the time by using the **+** or **−** buttons.

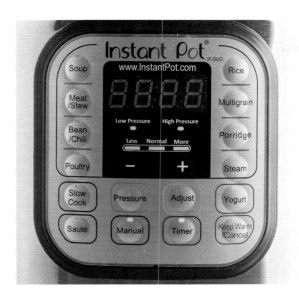

QUICK RELEASE VS. NATURAL RELEASE

Once the timer has gone off and the pressure cooking has finished, you have two choices on how to release the steam:

"Quick Release" is when you open the steam release handle by turning it from "Sealing" to "Venting" to let the steam release very quickly (just be careful of the steam; it's extremely hot and there will be a lot of it).

"Natural Release" is when the timer goes off and you let the pressure release without doing anything. When the pressure cooking time has finished, the Instant Pot automatically switches to the "Keep Warm" setting. During this time, the pressure begins to slowly drop. The amount of liquid and ingredients in the pot will determine how long this "Natural Release" process will take, but you can figure on at least 10 minutes and up to 20 minutes. Some recipes call for a "Natural Release" with a specific amount of time before venting the remaining steam.

ROOKIE MISTAKES

1. **Not setting the steam release valve to the locked position for pressure cooking and steaming.** If you don't lock it, pressure will never build.

2. **Not moving quickly enough.** When you open the steam release valve, do so in a very quick movement, or better yet, use a towel to release the valve because the steam escapes very quickly and it is extremely hot.

3. **Overfilling the pot.** It is best not to fill the pot more than two-thirds full (or one-half full for foods that expand, such as rice, pasta, and porridge), otherwise it could cause clogging, excess pressure, and leaking.

4. **Forgetting to add water for pressure cooking or steaming.** As a general rule, make it a habit to always fill your Instant Pot with 1½ cups (350 ml) of water and insert the steam rack before you do anything else.

5. **Not attaching the condensation collector.** This could result in water slowly leaking over your countertop through the night as your food slowly cooks.

6. **Touching the lid while pressure cooking.** That thing is hot!

7. **Remembering to turn off your Instant Pot.** Because the "Keep Warm/Cancel" button are the same, make sure to select the button when you finish preparing your meal. The display should switch to "Off."

Now that you understand how your Instant Pot works, it's time to get cooking! Here are the items that are great to have on hand when cooking with your Instant Pot, as well as when making the recipes in this book.

KITCHEN TOOLS

These are the kitchen tools that we have found to be especially useful when cooking with the Instant Pot.

ALUMINUM FOIL

Keep a roll handy because we ask you to use foil to cover the desserts before they go into the Instant Pot. We also use foil to make a "sling" that helps lower a tight-fitting dish into the Instant Pot and lift it out. To make a sling, tear off a 20-inch (51 cm) piece of foil and fold it over lengthwise into thirds (about 3 inches, or 7.5 cm, wide) to create a sturdy contraption that can be used multiple times.

METAL CAKE PANS

From the 6 x 3-inch (15 x 7.5 cm) round cake pan to the 7-inch (18 cm) tube and springform pans, these pans will suit your Instant Pot baking needs.

MEASURING CUPS

The Instant Pot contains lines of measurement, but we found it a little easier to use actual measuring cups when developing recipes and cooking.

SOUFFLÉ/CASSEROLE DISH

This versatile 8 x 3-inch (20 x 7.5 cm) round porcelain dish really maximizes the space in your Instant Pot, fitting in just perfectly with little room to spare.

STEAMER BASKET

This inexpensive steamer is different from the steam rack that is included with your Instant Pot. It has a collapsible basket that will expand to the size of your pot, maximizing the amount of vegetables you can steam. The holes are smaller, too, which means nothing will fall through.

TONGS

Tongs are one of the most efficient tools to have on hand. Use them to stir, turn, grab, pluck, and lift. We like the 9-inch (23 cm) size that locks closed for storage.

WOODEN SPOONS

Obviously, these are useful for all spoon-related reasons. But we particularly like a wooden spoon for scraping up the yummy brown bits from the bottom of the pot because it won't scratch it. Both rounded spoons and spoons that are squared off are recommended.

PANTRY ITEMS

These are the pantry items that are consistently used throughout this book. But these are also items that we use in our everyday cooking. You will find that most of these are basic things that you might already have in your kitchen.

BONE BROTH

More of a refrigerator or freezer staple, a bone broth is one of the most requested recipes for the Instant Pot. Whether you prefer to use it for cooking or for sipping.

CANNED CHIPOTLES IN ADOBO

Chipotle peppers are smoked and dried red jalapeños that have been rehydrated and canned in a tangy-sweet red sauce (adobo). If you are looking for a smoky taste with just a bit of heat, scrape the seeds out of the chiles or consider just using the sauce without any chiles at all. Once you open the can, you can store the chiles and sauce in an airtight container for a few weeks.

CHILI GARLIC SAUCE

This is a bright red, fiery sauce with nearly the same ingredients as sriracha, but it boasts a delicious garlicky taste and has bits of chopped chiles in it.

COCONUT MILK

Don't confuse coconut milk with coconut water, which comes from the center of green coconuts. Coconut milk is made from grating and pressing the "meat" of brown coconuts. It has a mildly sweet flavor and creamy texture. Make sure to vigorously shake the can before opening it to combine the thick cream with the watery milk.

CRUSHED RED PEPPER FLAKES

This is a blend of a variety of chiles that have been dried and crushed, not ground. Look for a jar containing bright red flakes. If they are dull in color, that means the peppers have begun to lose their flavor.

DRY RED AND WHITE WINE

Cooking with wine won't get you drunk. Actually, the alcohol evaporates during the cooking process and leaves a greater depth of flavor, which can sometimes be sweet or acidic. As a rule of thumb, only cook with wines that you would drink. For white, we reach for Sauvignon Blanc or Pinot Grigio, and for red, we reach for Cabernet Sauvignon or Merlot.

EXTRA-VIRGIN OLIVE OIL

We use this oil for everything, from sautéing meats and vegetables to making vinaigrettes, to drizzling over dips, soups, and stews just before serving. We prefer "first cold press," which means that it was made simply by pressing the olives.

FRESH HERBS

If you ever feel like your dish is missing something, reach for a fresh herb like parsley, dill, rosemary, or thyme. Folding in chopped fresh herbs to nearly any dish will transform the ordinary to extraordinary.

FRESH LEMON

This may be one of the best-kept pantry-staple secrets. We always have lemons in our produce drawer and not just for flavoring our water. Squeezing a bit of juice over a dish just before serving adds a bright finish. We also use fresh lemon juice in vinaigrettes, pastas, and even on roasted vegetables. But before you juice that lemon, grate some of the zest to add an extra zip to dips, casseroles, and rice.

FRESHLY GROUND BLACK PEPPER

Don't waste your money on pre-ground pepper; the taste barely resembles pepper at all. For the real deal, grind your own peppercorns in a pepper mill as needed. Our favorite black peppercorns are Tellicherry.

Or maybe you're experiencing the joy of owning an Air Fryer.

Instant Pot and Air Fryers are revolutionizing the way people cook at home. What would normally take a whole day of cooking and even more time in clean up can now be managed on a weeknight with these two fantastic appliances. Whether you have an Instant Pot or an Air Fryer independently or some combination of the two, the way you cook and experience food is about to drastically change. Air frying food gives all the delicious crisp and crunch to your favorite fried foods without all of the excess oil used for frying. It is a sure way to spice up any kitchen.

KITCHEN TOOLS
Along with the recommended tools for cooking with an Instant Pot, here are some additional things that will help you make the most out of your Air Fryer.

PARCHMENT CAKE ROUNDS
Lining the basket with pre-cut parchment rounds will save you time on prep and clean up.

SILICONE MUFFIN CUPS
Excellent for baking in your Air Fryer or for pre-portioning out your meals.

MEAT THERMOMETER
When coating meat in crispy toppings, it is especially helpful to know what the internal temperature of the meat is without having to cut individual pieces open.

MANDOLIN
This is a great tool for thinly slicing vegetables. It's especially helpful if you want to start air frying your own vegetable chips!

MICROPLANE
Great for grating fresh Parmesan on top of your favorite cheesy dishes or for zesting a lemon to add an extra pop of flavor.

RAMEKINS AND SMALL PYREX DISHES
Specific sizes of these will depend on the size of Air Fryer you have. If your Air Fryer is small, 6- to 7-inch (15 to 18 cm) dishes should work best.

SKEWERS
Bamboo or metal skewers work for the Air Fryer recipes. I use bamboo in the recipes, so if you use metal skewers use caution since they may be hot to the touch when you remove them from the Air Fryer.

PANTRY STAPLES
PANKO
Or any other type of favorite breadcrumb to help all your dishes get that satisfying crunch.

PARMESAN
Incorporating Parmesan with bread crumbs can add a dynamic combination of flavors.

OLIVE OIL COOKING SPRAY
Lubricating what you're cooking before you add it to your Air Fryer makes clean up as easy as cooking was.

DRIED SPICE MIX
Sometimes all you need to add to veggies are a few simple spices to really make them pop. Some different blends you could try are taco seasoning, jerk seasoning, everything bagel seasoning, or really any pre-mixed seasoning.

ROOKIE MISTAKES

1. Spraying the rack and not the food. Directly spraying the rack can damage the non-stick coating.

2. Crowding the Air Fryer. Give space around it for the air to escape while cooking.

3. Delaying clean up. If food residue is left to cool, it will stick and be MUCH harder to clean up afterwards.

4. Assuming that temperatures correlate to oven cooks. It's an entirely different appliance and best to err on the side of caution than to burn your dinner.

5. Thinking "Bigger is better!" Buy the right size for your home. They can be quite bulky, and there is no need to take up more counter space than is necessary.

6. Set it and forget it. Rotating food isn't always necessary, but for larger items you will want to flip them for the final few minutes of cooking to ensure everything is crisp and cooked on all sides.

BREAKFAST

Instant Pot

Yogurt Parfaits with Apricot-Glazed Berries

YIELD:
4 servings
PREP TIME:
20 minutes
COOK TIME:
8 hours 5 minutes (plus 6 hours refrigeration time)

INGREDIENTS

YOGURT
3¾ cups (880 ml) whole milk
4 teaspoons whole-milk plain Greek yogurt (we used Fage Total; you may use any yogurt that has live and active cultures)

PARFAITS
2 tablespoons (40 g) apricot jam
1 tablespoon (15 ml) fresh lemon juice
8 ounces (225 g) fresh strawberries, hulled and cut into pieces
6 ounces (170 g) fresh blueberries
1 cup (113 g) granola

NOTE: You can make more yogurt by using three 16-ounce (475 ml) canning jars (that is the most that can fit on the steamer rack without worry of it tipping over). Just fill the jars up, leaving about ½ inch (13 mm) at the top, and plan on a bit more refrigeration time.

1. To make the yogurt, insert the steam rack into the Instant Pot. Add 1½ cups (350 ml) water. Divide the milk among four 8-ounce (235 ml) canning jars and place on the rack. Place the jar lids (but not the rings) on top of each jar (covering them will ensure that no condensation or steam will drip into the jars).

2. Lock the lid and press [Steam] and cook for 1 minute. Use the "Natural Release" method for 5 minutes, then vent any remaining steam and open the lid.

3. Using oven mitts or canning tongs, carefully transfer the jars to a wire cooling rack and remove the lids (alternatively, leave the jars in the pot and carefully remove the lids). Let the milk cool, stirring occasionally, to 115°F (46°C). This will take at least 45 minutes (and likely double for 16-ounce, or 475 ml, jars; see Note left).

4. Once the milk in each jar has cooled to 115°F (46°C), spoon off and discard any skin that has formed on the top, then stir 1 teaspoon Greek yogurt into each jar. Place the jars back into the pot and cover with the lids (but not the rings). Lock the lid. Press [Yogurt] and cook for 8 hours. When it is finished, "Yogt" will appear on the display. Press [Cancel], then open the lid.

5. Remove the jars and use the rings to close the jars completely. Refrigerate until chilled, at least 6 hours or overnight.

6. To make the parfaits, in a medium bowl, whisk together the jam and lemon juice. Add the strawberries and blueberries and toss to coat.

7. In glasses or bowls, layer the yogurt with the granola and glazed berries.

Overnight 5-Grain Cereal with Raspberries and Coconut

YIELD:
4 servings
PREP TIME:
5 minutes
COOK TIME:
8 hours

INGREDIENTS

½ cup (40 g) steel-cut oats
¼ cup (50 g) pearl barley
¼ cup (46 g) millet
2 tablespoons (13 g) wheat bran
2 tablespoons (14 g) flaxseed meal
3½ cups (825 ml) water
½ teaspoon pure vanilla extract
½ teaspoon kosher salt

FOR SERVING
Fresh raspberries
Toasted coconut
Honey

1. In the Instant Pot, combine the oats, barley, millet, wheat bran, flaxseed meal, water, vanilla, and salt.

2. Lock the lid. Press [Slow Cook], leave the vent open, and cook on "More" for 8 hours.

3. Divide the cereal among bowls and top with raspberries, coconut, and honey.

Instant Pot

Shakshuka

YIELD:
2 servings
PREP TIME:
10 minutes
COOK TIME:
15 minutes

INGREDIENTS

2 tablespoons (30 ml)
  extra-virgin olive oil
1 medium yellow onion, sliced
1 red bell pepper, sliced
1 clove garlic, finely chopped
½ teaspoon ground cumin
½ teaspoon paprika
1 can (14½ ounces, or 410 g)
  diced tomatoes
½ teaspoon kosher salt,
  plus more for serving
¼ teaspoon freshly ground
  black pepper, plus more
  for serving
⅛ teaspoon crushed red
  pepper flakes
4 large eggs
1 tablespoon (4 g) chopped
  fresh flat-leaf parsley

1. Turn the Instant Pot on to [Sauté]. Heat the olive oil and add the onion and bell pepper, and cook, stirring often, until beginning to soften, 3 to 4 minutes. Add the garlic, cumin, and paprika, and cook, stirring, for 1 minute more.

2. Add the tomatoes, salt, black pepper, and red pepper flakes. Press [Cancel]. Lock the lid. Press [Manual] and cook on high pressure for 8 minutes. Use the "Quick Release" method to vent the steam, then open the lid.

3. Use a spoon to make a well in the sauce, then crack an egg into it. Repeat with the remaining eggs. Lock the lid. Press [Manual] and cook on high pressure for 1 minute (for soft yolks). Use the "Quick Release" method to vent the steam, press [Cancel], then open the lid.

4. Divide the eggs and sauce among plates and season the eggs with a little more salt and black pepper. Sprinkle with the parsley and serve.

Manual

Asparagus and Parmesan Frittata

YIELD:
4 servings
PREP TIME:
15 minutes
COOK TIME:
25 minutes

INGREDIENTS

Extra-virgin olive oil, for the pan
8 large eggs
½ cup (115 g) sour cream
¾ teaspoon kosher salt
½ teaspoon freshly ground
  black pepper
4 ounces (115 g) asparagus,
  trimmed and cut into ¼-inch
  (6 mm) pieces
2 scallions (white and light green
  parts), thinly sliced
2 tablespoons (8 g) chopped
  fresh flat-leaf parsley
¼ cup (25 g) plus 1 tablespoon
  (5 g) grated Parmesan cheese,
  divided

1. Insert the steam rack into the Instant Pot and add 1½ cups (350 ml) water. Oil a deep 6- to 7-inch (15 to 18 cm) round cake pan or soufflé dish.

2. In a large bowl, beat the eggs, sour cream, salt, and pepper. Mix in the asparagus, scallions, parsley, and ¼ cup (25 g) of the Parmesan.

3. Transfer the mixture to the prepared pan and place on top of the steam rack. Lock the lid. Press [Manual] and cook on high pressure for 12 minutes. Use the "Natural Release" method for 10 minutes, then vent any remaining steam and open the lid.

4. Preheat broiler. Sprinkle the remaining 1 tablespoon (5 g) Parmesan over the top and broil until golden brown.

Instant
Pot

Quinoa Breakfast Bowl with Broiled Tomatoes

YIELD:
4 servings
PREP TIME:
15 minutes
COOK TIME:
15 minutes

INGREDIENTS

1 cup (173 g) quinoa
1½ cups (350 ml) water
¾ teaspoon kosher salt, divided
1 pint cherry tomatoes
  (25 to 30 tomatoes)
1 tablespoon (15 ml) extra-virgin
  olive oil
¼ teaspoon freshly ground black
  pepper
2 scallions (white and light green
  parts), thinly sliced
2 tablespoons (8 g) chopped
  fresh flat-leaf parsley
1 avocado
2 large eggs, hard-boiled,
  cooled, and peeled

1. Using a fine-mesh strainer, rinse the quinoa, then place in the Instant Pot. Add the water and ½ teaspoon of the salt. Lock the lid. Press [Multigrain] and cook on high pressure for 7 minutes. Use the "Natural Release" method for 5 minutes, then vent any remaining steam and open the lid.

2. Fluff with a fork. Press [Cancel], lock the lid, and let sit for 5 minutes more.

3. While the quinoa is cooking, preheat broiler. On a small rimmed baking sheet, toss the tomatoes with the olive oil, pepper, and the remaining ¼ teaspoon salt. Broil until the tomatoes begin to burst, about 3 minutes. Toss with the scallions and parsley.

4. Pit, peel, and dice the avocado. Divide the quinoa among bowls, top with the tomatoes and avocado, then coarsely grate the eggs on top.

Sauté   Slow Cook

Butterscotch Pecan French Toast

YIELD:
4 servings
PREP TIME:
10 minutes
COOK TIME:
8 hours

INGREDIENTS

2 large eggs
1 cup (235 ml) half-and-half
1 teaspoon pure vanilla extract, divided
4 slices French or Italian bread, about 1 inch (2.5 cm) thick
3 tablespoons (45 g) unsalted butter
¾ cup (170 g) packed dark brown sugar
¼ cup (60 ml) heavy cream
½ cup (55 g) pecans, coarsely chopped
⅛ teaspoon kosher salt

1. In a large baking dish, whisk together the eggs, half-and-half, and ½ teaspoon of the vanilla. Add the bread slices and soak, flipping them halfway through, for about 5 minutes.

2. Turn the Instant Pot on to [Sauté]. Add the butter and melt. Add the brown sugar and whisk until melted, about 30 seconds. Press [Cancel]. Whisk in the cream until incorporated and smooth, then whisk in the pecans, salt, and the remaining ½ teaspoon vanilla.

3. Add the bread slices to the pot, shaking off extra egg mixture before you do. Overlap to fit as necessary. Lock the lid. Press [Slow Cook], leave the vent open, and cook on "More" for 8 hours.

4. Serve the French toast butterscotch side up. Drizzle the extra sauce and pecans over the top.

Instant
Pot

Banana Bread

YIELD:
6 servings
PREP TIME:
10 minutes
COOK TIME:
50 minutes

INGREDIENTS

¼ cup (½ stick, or 60 g) unsalted butter, melted, plus more for the pan

1 cup (120 g) all-purpose flour

½ teaspoon baking powder

¼ teaspoon baking soda

½ teaspoon kosher salt

⅛ teaspoon ground cinnamon, plus more for dusting

2 large eggs

⅓ cup (65 g) sugar

⅓ cup (77 g) sour cream

½ teaspoon pure vanilla extract

2 large ripe bananas, 1 mashed and 1 sliced, divided

½ cup (55 g) pecans, chopped

1 large ripe banana, sliced

1. Insert the steam rack into the Instant Pot and add 1½ cups (350 ml) water. Butter a 6 x 3-inch (15 x 7.5 cm) round cake pan.

2. In a medium bowl, whisk together the flour, baking powder, baking soda, salt, and cinnamon.

3. In a second medium bowl, whisk together the eggs, sugar, sour cream, melted butter, and vanilla. Mix in the mashed banana. Add the dry ingredients and mix to combine; stir in the pecans.

4. Scrape the batter into the prepared pan and cover with aluminum foil. Place the pan on the steam rack. Lock the lid.

5. Press [Manual] and cook on high pressure for 40 minutes. Use the "Quick Release" method to vent the steam, then open the lid.

6. Place the pan on a wire cooling rack and let cool for 10 minutes. Turn the bread out onto the rack and let cool completely. To serve, top with the sliced banana and dust with cinnamon.

Breakfast Chimichanga

YIELD:
2 servings
PREP TIME:
20 minutes
COOK TIME:
17 minutes

INGREDIENTS

- 1 tablespoon (15 ml) extra-virgin olive oil
- ½ medium onion, chopped
- ½ bell pepper, chopped
- 1 jalapeño, finely chopped
- ½ teaspoon kosher salt, divided
- ⅓ cup (80 g) refried beans
- 2 extra-large tortillas
- 1 small avocado, peeled, pitted, and sliced
- ⅓ cup (40 g) grated extra-sharp Cheddar cheese
- 3 large eggs, lightly beaten

1. Heat the oil in a large nonstick skillet over medium heat. Add the onion, bell pepper, jalapeño, and ¼ teaspoon of the salt and cook, stirring occasionally, until the vegetables are tender and starting to turn golden, 8 to 10 minutes.

2. Meanwhile, divide the refried beans between the two tortillas, spreading into an even rectangular shape in the center. Top with the avocado slices and cheese. Spoon the cooked onion and pepper on top.

3. Return the skillet to medium heat, add the eggs to the skillet, and scramble, stirring occasionally, until cooked through, 2 to 3 minutes. Spoon on top of the onion and pepper.

4. Roll the burritos. Fold both of the short sides of the tortillas in toward the center. Starting on one long side, roll up the tortilla and place seam-side down on the Air Fryer rack. Cook at 390°F (200°C) until crisp and golden brown, about 4 minutes.

Spanish Breakfast Potatoes

YIELD:
2 servings
PREP TIME:
10 minutes
COOK TIME:
30 minutes

INGREDIENTS

SAUCE
2 tablespoons (30 ml) extra-
    virgin olive oil
1 small onion, diced
Pinch of kosher salt
3 cloves garlic, thinly sliced
1 teaspoon smoked paprika
1 can (14 ounces, or 392 g)
    whole tomatoes

POTATOES
2 medium russet potatoes
2 teaspoons extra-virgin olive oil,
    plus more for greasing
¼ teaspoon kosher salt
¼ teaspoon freshly ground
    black pepper
2 large eggs

1. To make the sauce: Heat the oil in a large skillet. Add the onion and a pinch of salt, and cook, stirring, until tender, 5 to 7 minutes.

2. Add the garlic and cook for another minute. Add the paprika, stir, then add the tomatoes and break up using a wooden spoon. Simmer gently for 15 minutes, then season to taste.

3. To make the potatoes: Meanwhile, peel and cut the potatoes into ½-inch (1.3 cm)-thick wedges. Transfer to a large bowl and toss with the olive oil, salt, and pepper. Transfer to the Air Fryer rack and cook at 400°F (205°C) until golden and tender, 15 to 17 minutes, shaking the rack halfway through cooking. Remove from the Air Fryer.

4. For the eggs, grease a 6- to 7-inch (15 to 18 cm) aluminum pan and crack the eggs inside. Transfer to the Air Fryer rack and cook at 370°F (190°C) for 5 to 7 minutes, or until the eggs are cooked to your desired doneness. Serve the potatoes with the sauce and eggs.

Spinach & Goat Cheese Frittatas

YIELD:
6 frittatas
PREP TIME:
15 minutes
COOK TIME:
12 minutes

INGREDIENTS

- 2 teaspoons extra-virgin olive oil
- 1 clove garlic, finely chopped
- 5 ounces (140 g) baby spinach
- 4 large eggs
- ¼ teaspoon kosher salt
- ¼ teaspoon freshly ground black pepper
- 2 ounces (56 g) goat cheese, crumbled

1. Heat the oil in a large skillet. Add the garlic and cook, stirring, until starting to turn golden, 1 to 2 minutes. Add the spinach and cook, stirring, until just wilted. Remove from the skillet and pat dry. Roughly chop.

2. Crack the eggs into a medium bowl and beat with the salt and pepper until evenly broken up. Fold in the spinach and cheese.

3. Divide the mixture among 6 silicone muffin cups (about ¼ cup [60 ml] each) and transfer to the Air Fryer rack. Cook at 300°F (150°C) until puffed, golden, and just set, about 10 minutes.

APPETIZERS

Instant
Pot

YIELD:
12 pieces
PREP TIME:
20 minutes
COOK TIME:
6 minutes

Deviled Eggs

INGREDIENTS

6 large eggs
¼ cup (60 g) mayonnaise
1 tablespoon (15 ml) fresh
   lemon juice
1 teaspoon Dijon mustard
⅛ teaspoon freshly ground
   black pepper
Toppings: crumbled cooked
   bacon, chopped fresh herbs,
   sliced scallions or green beans,
   and ground spices such as
   cumin, curry powder, or
   smoked paprika

1. Insert the steam rack into the Instant Pot and add 1½ cups (350 ml) water. Place 6 small canning jar rings or metal cookie cutters (any shape will work as long as the egg can sit inside) on the steam rack and place an egg in each one (this will keep them from rolling around).

2. Lock the lid. Press [Manual] and cook on low pressure for 6 minutes.

3. Use the "Quick Release" method to vent the steam, then open the lid. Immediately transfer the eggs to a bowl of ice water to cool.

4. In a medium bowl, whisk together the mayonnaise, lemon juice, mustard, and pepper.

5. Peel the eggs and slice them in half lengthwise. Scoop the yolks into the mayonnaise mixture and mash to combine. Spoon the mixture into the whites and sprinkle with desired toppings.

Instant Pot

Smoky Glazed Chicken Wings

YIELD:
4 servings
PREP TIME:
15 minutes
COOK TIME:
15 minutes

INGREDIENTS

- 2 pounds (907 g) chicken wings, cut in half at the joint (about 24 pieces total)
- 1 teaspoon ground cumin
- 1 teaspoon ground coriander
- 1 teaspoon paprika
- 2 cans (6 ounces, or 175 ml, each) pineapple juice, divided
- 2 canned chipotle chiles in adobo sauce, finely chopped, plus 1 tablespoon (15 ml) adobo sauce
- 2 tablespoons (40 g) honey
- 1 tablespoon (11 g) Dijon mustard
- 1 lime, cut into wedges, for serving

1. In a large bowl, toss the chicken wings with the cumin, coriander, and paprika.

2. Insert the steam rack into the Instant Pot and add all but ¼ cup (60 ml) of the pineapple juice. Evenly arrange the wings in the pot, standing them on end, if necessary.

3. Lock the lid. Press [Manual] and cook on high pressure for 8 minutes. Use the "Quick Release" method to vent the steam, then open the lid.

4. While the chicken is cooking, preheat broiler and line a large rimmed baking sheet with aluminum foil. In a large bowl, whisk together the chiles, adobo sauce, honey, mustard, and the reserved pineapple juice.

5. Transfer the wings to the bowl with the sauce and toss to coat. Arrange them in a single layer on the prepared baking sheet and broil until beginning to char, about 3 minutes per side. Serve with the lime wedges for squeezing over the wings.

Instant Pot

Hummus with Olives, Cucumbers, and Tomatoes

YIELD:
4 servings
PREP TIME:
10 minutes
COOK TIME:
1 hour

INGREDIENTS

1 cup (250 g) dried chickpeas, rinsed
2 cloves garlic, peeled
¼ cup (60 g) sesame tahini
¼ cup (60 ml) fresh lemon juice
1¼ teaspoons kosher salt
1 teaspoon ground cumin
½ cup (120 ml) extra-virgin olive oil
¼ cup (60 ml) warm water

FOR SERVING
Kalamata olives
Diced cucumber
Diced tomato
Pita chips

1. In the Instant Pot, combine the chickpeas and 4 cups (950 ml) water. Lock the lid. Press [Manual] and cook on high pressure for 45 minutes. Use the "Natural Release" method for 15 minutes, then vent any remaining steam and open the lid. Drain the chickpeas into a strainer and rinse under cold water to cool.

2. In a food processor, chop the garlic. Add the chickpeas, tahini, lemon juice, salt, and cumin. Process until a thick paste forms. With the motor running, slowly drizzle in the olive oil and let run until thick and creamy. Then drizzle in the water and purée until smooth and very creamy.

3. Spoon the hummus into a bowl and top with olives, cucumber, and tomato. Serve with pita chips.

Instant
Pot

Sauté   Manual

Caramelized Onion Dip

YIELD:
1½ cups (375 g)
PREP TIME:
10 minutes
COOK TIME:
20 minutes

INGREDIENTS

- 2 tablespoons (30 g) unsalted butter
- 2 medium yellow onions, thinly sliced
- ¾ teaspoon kosher salt, divided
- 1 cup (230 g) sour cream
- ½ teaspoon Worcestershire sauce
- 3 fresh chives
- Freshly ground black pepper, to taste
- Potato chips, for serving

1. Turn the Instant Pot on to [Sauté]. Melt the butter, then add the onions and ½ teaspoon of the salt, and stir to coat. Press [Cancel]. Lock the lid. Press [Manual] and cook on high pressure for 10 minutes. Use the "Quick Release" method to vent the steam, then open the lid.

2. Press [Sauté] and cook, stirring occasionally with a wooden spoon to scrape up the brown bits from the bottom of the pot, until the liquid has cooked away and the onions turn a golden brown, about 10 minutes. Transfer to a medium bowl and refrigerate until completely cool.

3. To the onions, add the sour cream, Worcestershire, and the remaining ¼ teaspoon salt, and stir well to combine. Using kitchen scissors, snip the chives into small pieces over the top and season with pepper. Serve with potato chips.

Instant Pot

Chorizo and Pinto Bean Nachos

YIELD:
4 servings
PREP TIME:
20 minutes
COOK TIME:
1 hour

INGREDIENTS

1 small red onion
1 tablespoon (15 ml) extra-virgin olive oil
8 ounces (225 g) fresh Mexican chorizo, casings removed
2 cloves garlic, finely chopped
½ teaspoon ground cumin
1 cup (250 g) dried pinto beans, rinsed
2½ cups (595 ml) water
3 tablespoons (45ml) fresh lime juice
¼ teaspoon kosher salt
¼ teaspoon freshly ground black pepper
6 ounces (170 g) tortilla chips
1½ cups shredded pepper Jack cheese (about 4 ounces, or 115 g)
6 radishes, thinly sliced
1 jalapeño, thinly sliced
½ cup (8 g) coarsely chopped fresh cilantro
Sour cream, for serving

1. Finely chop half the onion. Turn the Instant Pot on to [Sauté]. Heat the olive oil. Add the chopped onion and chorizo, and cook, breaking up the chorizo into small pieces with a spoon and stirring occasionally until no longer pink, about 4 minutes.

2. Add the garlic and cumin and cook, stirring, for 1 minute. Add the beans and water. Press [Cancel]. Lock the lid. Press [Manual] and cook on high pressure for 35 minutes. Use the "Natural Release" method for 15 minutes, then vent any remaining steam and open the lid.

3. While the beans are cooking, thinly slice the remaining half onion and toss in a small bowl with the lime juice, salt, and pepper. Let sit, tossing occasionally, until ready to use.

4. Preheat broiler and line a large rimmed baking sheet with aluminum foil.

5. Arrange half the tortilla chips on the prepared baking sheet. Top with one-third of the cheese, then half the beans and another one-third of the cheese. Top with the remaining chips, beans, and cheese, and broil until the cheese melts, about 3 minutes.

6. Toss the onions with the radishes, jalapeño, and cilantro, then scatter over the nachos. Dollop with sour cream.

Instant
Pot

Sweet-and-Sour Cocktail Meatballs

YIELD:
22 meatballs
PREP TIME:
20 minutes
COOK TIME:
10 minutes

INGREDIENTS

MEATBALLS
1 pound (454 g) ground pork
or chicken
4 scallions (white and light green
parts), finely chopped, plus
more for serving
2 tablespoons (16 g) finely
grated fresh ginger
1 tablespoon (15 ml)
less-sodium soy sauce
1 large egg white
½ teaspoon kosher salt

SAUCE
½ cup (120 ml) fresh
orange juice
½ cup (120 ml) rice vinegar
¼ cup (50 g) sugar
5 to 6 teaspoons chili-garlic
sauce
2 tablespoons (16 g) cornstarch
2 tablespoons (30 ml) water

1. To make the meatballs, in a large bowl, combine the pork, scallions, ginger, soy sauce, egg white, and salt. Mix with your hands until evenly incorporated. Using wet hands, shape the mixture into 22 small balls.

2. To make the sauce, in the Instant Pot, whisk together the orange juice, vinegar, sugar, and chili-garlic paste. Press [Sauté] and bring the sauce to a boil. In a small bowl, whisk together the cornstarch and water. Once the sauce comes to a boil, slowly whisk in the cornstarch mixture. Press [Cancel]. Continue to whisk until the sauce stops boiling.

3. Add the meatballs to the sauce in a single layer. Lock the lid. Press [Manual] and cook on high pressure for 3 minutes. Use the "Quick Release" method to vent the steam, then open the lid.

4. Serve the meatballs and sauce sprinkled with scallions.

Instant Pot

Vegetable Pot Stickers with Sesame-Ginger Dipping Sauce

Sauté   Steam

YIELD:
30 pot stickers
PREP TIME:
45 minutes
COOK TIME:
20 minutes

INGREDIENTS

POT STICKERS
5 tablespoons (75 ml) canola oil, divided
8 ounces (225 g) shiitake mushrooms, caps sliced, stems discarded
1 tablespoon (15 ml) less-sodium soy sauce
3 scallions (white and light green parts), thinly sliced
1 small bunch of kale, thick stems and inner ribs discarded, leaves torn into pieces (about 6 cups, or 400 g)
½ teaspoon kosher salt
1 medium carrot, grated
30 square wonton wrappers
¾ cup (180 ml) water, divided

DIPPING SAUCE
½ cup (120 ml) less-sodium soy sauce
⅓ cup (80 ml) rice vinegar
2 tablespoons (30 ml) hot pepper sesame oil or toasted sesame oil
2 tablespoons (16 g) finely grated fresh ginger
2 teaspoons packed dark brown sugar

1. To make the filling, in a large skillet, heat 2 tablespoons (30 ml) of the canola oil over medium-high heat. Add the mushrooms and cook, stirring often, until tender, 3 to 4 minutes. Stir in the soy sauce and scallions. Add the kale and salt, and stir to coat. Reduce the heat to medium, cover tightly, and cook, stirring occasionally, until tender, 3 to 4 minutes. Stir in the carrot. Let cool.

2. To form the pot stickers, place a heaping teaspoon of the filling into the center of a wonton wrapper. Moisten the edges with water, fold over into a triangle, and press the edges tightly together to seal. Repeat with the remaining filling and wrappers.

3. To make the dipping sauce, in a small bowl, stir together the soy sauce, vinegar, sesame oil, ginger, and brown sugar.

4. Turn the Instant Pot on to [Sauté]. Heat 1 tablespoon (15 ml) of the canola oil. Add a single layer of pot stickers (you should be able to fit 10) and cook until the undersides are golden brown, about 1 minute. Press [Cancel].

5. Add ¼ cup (60 ml) of the water. Lock the lid. Press [Steam] and cook for 3 minutes. Use the "Quick Release" method to release the steam, then open the lid. Transfer to a plate. Wipe out the pot and repeat steps 4 and 5 two more times with the remaining pot stickers, canola oil, and water.

6. Serve the pot stickers with the dipping sauce.

Air Fryer

Cheesy Garlic and Herb Stuffed Mushrooms

YIELD:
4 servings
PREP TIME:
10 minutes
COOK TIME:
9 minutes

INGREDIENTS

- 8 ounces (227 g) medium cremini mushrooms, brushed clean
- 2 ounces (56 g) garlic and herb soft cheese (such as Boursin)
- 2 tablespoons (14 g) panko bread crumbs

1. Remove the stems from the mushrooms and discard. Fill each mushroom cap with ½ to 1 teaspoon (depending on the size of the mushroom) of the cheese and sprinkle with the panko bread crumbs.

2. Place the mushrooms on the Air Fryer rack and cook at 360°F (185°C) until the mushrooms are tender and the tops golden brown, about 9 minutes.

Everything Bagel Mozzarella Sticks

Air Fry

YIELD:
4 servings
PREP TIME:
15 minutes. plus 1 hour freezing
COOK TIME:
8 minutes

INGREDIENTS

3 tablespoons (24 g) all-purpose flour
¼ teaspoon salt
½ teaspoon dried oregano
1 large egg
½ cup (60 g) panko bread crumbs
1 tablespoon (6 g) everything bagel seasoning
4 mozzarella sticks

1. In a shallow bowl or pie dish, whisk together the flour, salt, and oregano. In a second shallow bowl or pie dish, lightly beat the egg. In a third shallow bowl or pie dish, combine the panko bread crumbs with the everything bagel seasoning.

2. Working with one mozzarella stick at a time, coat the stick in the flour, then coat in the egg, tapping off the excess, and finally roll in the panko mixture.

3. Transfer to a plate and freeze for at least 1 hour. Reserve the remaining ingredients while the mozzarella sticks chill.

4. Coat the mozzarella sticks for a second time, first in the flour, then the egg, and finally the panko mixture. Transfer to the Air Fryer rack and cook at 390°F (200°C) until golden brown, 6 to 8 minutes.

Air Fry

Avocado Fries

YIELD:
4 servings
PREP TIME:
20 minutes
COOK TIME:
8 minutes

INGREDIENTS

FRIES
1 large egg
¾ cup (90 g) panko bread crumbs
¼ cup (25 g) grated
   Parmesan cheese
¼ teaspoon kosher salt
¼ teaspoon freshly ground
   black pepper
1 large avocado, peeled,
   seeded, and sliced ¼ inch
   (6 mm) thick
Juice of ½ lime

SAUCE
2 teaspoons sriracha
¼ cup (60 g) mayonnaise

1. To make the fries: In a shallow bowl or pie dish, lightly beat the egg. In a second shallow bowl or pie dish, combine the panko, Parmesan, salt, and pepper.

2. Working with one slice at a time, coat the avocado slices in the egg. Use a fork to remove any excess, then coat generously in the panko mixture. Repeat with the remaining slices.

3. Place the avocado slices on the Air Fryer rack in an even layer, not overlapping. Cook at 400°F (205°C) until golden brown, 7 to 8 minutes, turning once after 4 minutes. Once cooked, transfer to a serving dish and squeeze over the lime juice.

4. To make the sauce: Meanwhile, in a small bowl, swirl the sriracha through the mayonnaise. Serve with the fries.

Air Fry

Cheese Puffs

YIELD:
4 to 6 servings
PREP TIME:
20 minutes
COOK TIME:
20 minutes

INGREDIENTS

1 ounce (28 g) goat cheese
¼ cup (56 g) unsalted butter
3 ounces (84 g) extra-sharp
   Cheddar cheese, coarsely
   grated
1 large egg white
4 ounces (112 g) country white
   bread, sliced into 1-inch
   (2.5 cm) cubes

1. In a medium saucepan, combine the goat cheese, butter, and Cheddar and melt over low heat until smooth.

2. In a medium bowl, whisk the egg white until stiff. Gently fold into the cheese mixture.

3. Coat the bread cubes in the cheese mixture.

4. Transfer half of the bread cubes to the Air Fryer rack and cook at 390°F (200°C) for 6 minutes. Flip and continue cooking until puffed and golden brown, 2 to 4 minutes longer.

5. Transfer to a serving platter and cook the remaining cheese puffs.

Crispy Spiced Chickpeas

YIELD:
1½ cups (360 g)
PREP TIME:
10 minutes
COOK TIME:
20 minutes

INGREDIENTS

2 teaspoons extra-virgin olive oil
1 teaspoon ground cumin
1 teaspoon sesame seeds
1 teaspoon chili powder
½ teaspoon dried thyme
¼ teaspoon garlic powder
¼ teaspoon kosher salt
1 can (15 ounces, or 420 g) chickpeas, drained, rinsed, and patted dry

1. In a medium bowl, combine the olive oil, cumin, sesame seeds, chili powder, thyme, garlic powder, and salt. Toss with the chickpeas to coat. Discard any skins that come off.

2. Transfer the chickpeas to the Air Fryer rack and cook at 370°F (190°C), shaking the basket every 5 minutes, until crispy, 18 to 20 minutes.

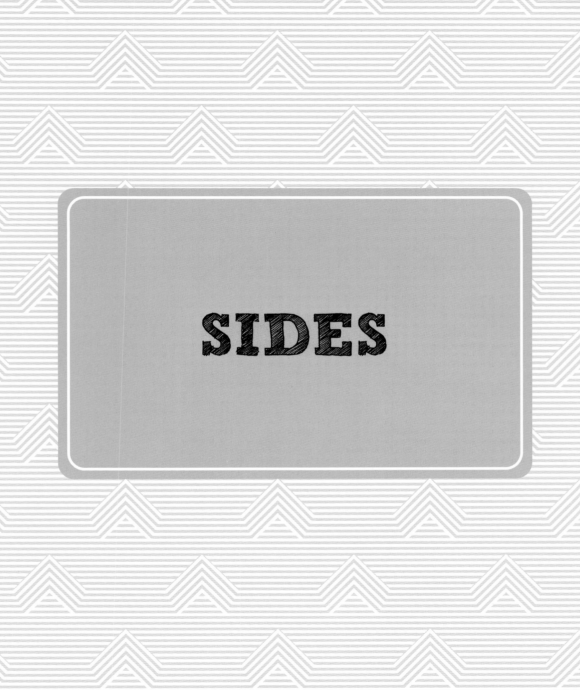

SIDES

Instant Pot

Manual

Potato Salad with Mustard Vinaigrette

YIELD:
4 to 6 servings
PREP TIME:
15 minutes
COOK TIME:
8 minutes

INGREDIENTS

2 pounds (907 g) small new potatoes (about 16)
3 tablespoons (45 ml) extra-virgin olive oil
2 tablespoons (30 ml) red wine vinegar
1 tablespoon (11 g) whole-grain mustard
2 teaspoons Dijon mustard
2 half-sour pickles, cut into small pieces, plus 1 tablespoon (15 ml) brine
½ teaspoon kosher salt
¼ teaspoon freshly ground black pepper
½ medium red onion, thinly sliced
⅓ cup (20 g) coarsely chopped fresh flat-leaf parsley

1. Insert the steam rack or steamer basket into the Instant Pot and add 1½ cups (350 ml) water. Place the potatoes on top of the basket and lock the lid. Press [Manual] and cook on high pressure for 8 minutes. Use the "Quick Release" method to vent the steam, then open the lid. Transfer the potatoes to a colander and run under cold water until cool enough to handle.

2. In a large bowl, whisk together the oil, vinegar, mustards, brine, salt, and pepper, then stir in the onion.

3. Cut each potato into quarters, transfer to the bowl with the vinaigrette, and toss to coat. Add the pickles and parsley, and toss to combine.

Instant Pot

Manual | Sauté

Spaghetti Squash with Garlic and Sage Brown Butter

YIELD:
4 servings
PREP TIME:
10 minutes
COOK TIME:
20 minutes

INGREDIENTS

1 spaghetti squash (about 3½ pounds, or 1.6 kg), halved crosswise and seeded
2 teaspoons packed light brown sugar
¼ teaspoon kosher salt
⅛ teaspoon freshly ground black pepper
⅛ teaspoon crushed red pepper flakes
¼ cup (½ stick, or 60 g) unsalted butter
2 cloves garlic, thinly sliced
12 fresh sage leaves

1. Insert the steam rack into the Instant Pot. Add 1½ cups (350 ml) water.

2. Place the spaghetti squash halves on the steam rack. Lock the lid. Press [Manual] and cook on high pressure for 15 minutes. Use the "Quick Release" method to vent the steam, then open the lid. Press [Cancel].

3. In a small bowl, combine the brown sugar, salt, black pepper, and red pepper flakes. Set aside.

4. Lift out the squash. Using 2 forks, shred the squash into long strands and place on a large plate.

5. Pour out the water and dry the pot. Press [Sauté]. Melt the butter in the pot. Add the garlic and cook, stirring constantly, until light golden brown, about 1½ minutes. Add the sage and the brown sugar mixture and cook, stirring, until the sage is crisp, about 45 seconds.

6. Lift out the inner pot, spoon the sauce over the squash, and serve.

Instant Pot

Twice-Baked Potatoes with Broccoli and Cheddar

YIELD:
4 servings
PREP TIME:
15 minutes
COOK TIME:
50 minutes

INGREDIENTS

- 4 russet potatoes (about 12 ounces, or 340 g, each)
- 1 bag (10 ounces, or 280 g) frozen broccoli, thawed and coarsely chopped
- 2 scallions (white and light green parts), finely chopped
- 1 cup (115 g) shredded Cheddar cheese, plus more for sprinkling
- 1 cup (230 g) sour cream
- ¾ teaspoon kosher salt
- ¼ teaspoon freshly ground black pepper

1. Insert the steam rack into the Instant Pot. Add 1½ cups (350 ml) water.

2. Pierce the potatoes several times with a fork and place them on the steam rack. Lock the lid. Press [Manual] and cook on high pressure for 25 minutes. Use the "Natural Release" method for 15 minutes, then vent any remaining steam and open the lid.

3. Preheat oven to 450°F (230°C, or gas mark 8).

4. When cool enough to handle, make a slit in the top of each potato and carefully scoop out the potato flesh into a medium bowl, keeping the potato skin intact.

5. Mash the potatoes. Fold in the broccoli, scallions, Cheddar, sour cream, salt, and pepper. Spoon the mixture back into the potato skins and place on a rimmed baking sheet.

6. Sprinkle the tops with a little more cheese. Bake until the Cheddar melts and the filling is hot throughout, about 10 minutes.

Instant
Pot

Spice-Rubbed Cauliflower Steaks

YIELD:
4 servings
PREP TIME:
10 minutes
COOK TIME:
5 minutes

INGREDIENTS

1 large head cauliflower (about
  2 pounds, or 907 g)
2 tablespoons (30 ml) extra-
  virgin olive oil
2 teaspoons paprika
2 teaspoons ground cumin
¾ teaspoon kosher salt
¼ cup (4 g) chopped fresh
  cilantro
1 lemon, quartered

1. Insert the steam rack into the Instant Pot. Add 1½ cups
   (350 ml) water.

2. Remove the leaves from the cauliflower and trim the core so
   the cauliflower sits flat. Place on the steam rack.

3. In a small bowl, combine the olive oil, paprika, cumin, and salt.
   Drizzle over the cauliflower and rub to coat.

4. Lock the lid. Press [Manual] and cook on high pressure for
   4 minutes. Use the "Quick Release" method to vent the steam,
   then open the lid.

5. Lift the cauliflower onto a cutting board and slice into 1-inch-
   thick (2.5 cm) steaks. Divide among plates and sprinkle with
   the cilantro. Serve with the lemon quarters.

Instant
Pot

Creamy Rice with Poblanos and Corn

YIELD:
4 servings
PREP TIME:
15 minutes
COOK TIME:
20 minutes

INGREDIENTS

- 2 tablespoons (30 ml) extra-virgin olive oil
- 1 medium yellow onion, finely chopped
- 1 poblano chile, seeded and cut into ¼-inch (6 mm) pieces
- ½ teaspoon kosher salt
- ¼ teaspoon freshly ground black pepper
- 2 cloves garlic, finely chopped
- 1½ cups (293 g) long-grain white rice
- 1½ cups (350 ml) water
- 1 cup (163 g) fresh corn kernels
- 1 cup (230 g) sour cream
- ¼ cup (60 ml) fresh lime juice
- ½ cup (8 g) chopped fresh cilantro

1. Turn the Instant Pot on to [Sauté]. Heat the olive oil. Add the onion, poblano, salt, and pepper, and cook, stirring occasionally, for 5 minutes. Add the garlic and cook, stirring, for 1 minute. Press [Cancel].

2. Stir in the rice and water. Lock the lid. Press [Manual] and cook on high pressure for 3 minutes. Use the "Natural Release" method for 10 minutes, then vent the remaining steam and open the lid.

3. Stir in the corn and cook for 1 minute. Press [Cancel]. Fold in the sour cream and lime juice, then fold in the cilantro. Serve immediately.

Instant Pot

Sauté Manual

Mexican Black Beans

YIELD:
4 servings
PREP TIME:
15 minutes
COOK TIME:
35 minutes

INGREDIENTS

¼ bunch fresh cilantro
1 tablespoon (15 ml) extra-virgin olive oil
1 large onion, finely chopped
½ teaspoon kosher salt
½ teaspoon freshly ground black pepper
4 cloves garlic, finely chopped
1 teaspoon ground cumin
1 teaspoon dried oregano
1½ cups (375 g) dried black beans, rinsed
3 cups (700 ml) water
2 tablespoons (30 ml) sherry vinegar
Sliced scallions, for serving
Crumbled queso fresco, for serving

1. Finely chop the cilantro stems. Turn the Instant Pot on to [Sauté]. Heat the olive oil and add the onion, salt, and pepper, and cook, stirring occasionally, for 5 minutes. Stir in the garlic, cumin, oregano, and cilantro stems, and cook for 1 minute.

2. Add the beans and water. Press [Cancel]. Lock the lid. Press [Manual] and cook on high pressure for 25 minutes.

3. Use the "Natural Release" method for 5 minutes, then vent any remaining steam and open the lid. Stir in the vinegar.

4. Transfer to a serving bowl and sprinkle with the scallions and cheese.

Instant Pot

Smashed Root Vegetables

YIELD:
6 servings
PREP TIME:
15 minutes
COOK TIME:
20 minutes

INGREDIENTS

6 sprigs fresh thyme
2 sprigs fresh rosemary
6 cloves garlic, peeled
8 ounces (225 g) carrots,
   peeled and cut into 1-inch
   (2.5 cm) pieces
8 ounces (225 g) parsnips,
   peeled and cut into 1-inch
   (2.5 cm) pieces
12 ounces (340 g) rutabaga,
   peeled and cut into 1-inch
   (2.5 cm) pieces
1 pound (455 g) Yukon gold
   potatoes (about 4), peeled
   and quartered
¼ cup (60 ml) extra-virgin olive
   oil, plus more for drizzling
¾ teaspoon kosher salt
¼ teaspoon freshly ground black
   pepper, plus more for serving

1. Place the thyme and rosemary in the bottom of the Instant Pot. Insert the steam rack into the pot and add 1½ cups (350 ml) water. Arrange the garlic, carrots on the rack, then top with the parsnips and rutabaga, followed by the potatoes.

2. Lock the lid. Press [Manual] and cook on high pressure for 10 minutes. Use the "Natural Release" method for 10 minutes, then vent any remaining steam and open the lid.

3. Transfer the vegetables to a bowl and coarsely mash together with the olive oil, salt, and pepper.

4. Drizzle with a little more olive oil, sprinkle with more pepper, and serve.

Instant Pot

Three-Bean Salad

YIELD:
4 servings
PREP TIME:
15 minutes
COOK TIME:
50 minutes

INGREDIENTS

¾ cup (188 g) dried kidney
   beans, rinsed

¾ cup (188 g) dried cannellini
   beans, rinsed

2 bay leaves

¼ cup (60 ml) fresh lemon juice

¼ cup (60 ml) extra-virgin olive oil

1 teaspoon chopped fresh
   rosemary

¾ teaspoon kosher salt

¼ teaspoon freshly ground
   black pepper

2 ribs celery, finely chopped

½ medium red onion, finely
   chopped

8 ounces (225 g) green beans,
   trimmed and cut into ¼-inch
   (6 mm) pieces

¼ cup (15 g) finely chopped fresh
   flat-leaf parsley

1. Place the kidney beans, cannellini beans, and bay leaves in the Instant Pot along with 7 cups (1.6 L) water. Lock the lid. Press [Manual] and cook on high pressure for 30 minutes.

2. While the beans are cooking, in a large bowl, whisk together the lemon juice, olive oil, rosemary, salt, and pepper to make the vinaigrette. Add the celery and onion, and toss to combine.

3. Use the "Natural Release" method for 15 minutes, then vent any remaining steam and open the lid. Discard the bay leaves. Add the green beans and let stand for 5 minutes.

4. Drain the beans and run them under cold water to cool. Add them to the bowl with the celery and onion. Add the parsley and toss everything in the vinaigrette to combine.

Instant Pot

Scallion Corn Bread

YIELD:
6 servings
PREP TIME:
10 minutes
COOK TIME:
40 minutes

INGREDIENTS

6 tablespoons (85 g) unsalted butter, melted, plus more for the pan and for serving
1 cup (125 g) all-purpose flour
½ cup (70 g) finely ground cornmeal
¼ cup (50 g) sugar
½ teaspoon baking powder
¼ teaspoon baking soda
½ teaspoon kosher salt
1 large egg
¾ cup (180 ml) buttermilk
1 scallion (white and light green parts), finely chopped

1. Insert the steam rack into the Instant Pot. Add 1½ cups (350 ml) water.

2. Butter a 6 x 3-inch (15 x 7.5 cm) round cake pan. In a medium bowl, whisk together the flour, cornmeal, sugar, baking powder, baking soda, and salt.

3. In a large bowl, beat the egg, then whisk in the buttermilk and melted butter. Add the flour mixture to the egg mixture and mix until fully incorporated, then fold in the scallion.

4. Scrape the batter into the prepared pan and cover with aluminum foil. Place the pan on the steam rack.

5. Lock the lid. Press [Manual] and cook on high pressure for 35 minutes. Use the "Quick Release" method to vent the steam, then open the lid. Transfer the pan to a wire cooling rack and let cool for 5 minutes. Serve warm with butter.

Air Fryer

Air Fry

Asian Roasted Broccoli

YIELD:
2 servings
PREP TIME:
4 minutes
COOK TIME:
12 minutes

INGREDIENTS

1 teaspoon soy sauce
1 teaspoon of chili garlic sauce
1 teaspoon extra-virgin olive oil
1 teaspoon brown sugar
1 teaspoon rice vinegar
½ teaspoon sesame oil
8 ounces (227 g) broccoli florets
Squeeze of fresh lemon juice
2 tablespoons (18 g) chopped
    roasted peanuts

1. In a large bowl, combine the soy sauce, chili garlic sauce, olive oil, brown sugar, rice vinegar, and sesame oil. Toss the broccoli in the mixture so that it is fully coated.

2. Transfer the broccoli to the Air Fryer rack and cook at 370°F (190°C) until golden brown and firm-tender, 10 to 12 minutes.

3. Transfer to a serving bowl, squeeze over the lemon, and sprinkle with the peanuts to serve.

Air Fryer

Brussel Sprouts with Hazelnuts and Parmesan

YIELD:
4 servings
PREP TIME:
10 minutes
COOK TIME:
17 minutes

INGREDIENTS

- 1 pound (454 g) Brussels sprouts, trimmed and quartered
- 1 tablespoon (15 ml) extra-virgin olive oil
- ¼ teaspoon kosher salt
- ¼ teaspoon freshly ground black pepper
- ¼ cup (35 g) chopped hazelnuts
- 2 tablespoons (10 g) grated Parmesan
- 1 teaspoon finely grated lemon zest
- 1 tablespoon (15 ml) fresh lemon juice

1. In a large bowl, toss the Brussels sprouts with the olive oil, salt, and pepper.

2. Transfer to the Air Fryer rack and cook at 380°F (195°C) until tender and starting to turn golden, about 15 minutes.

3. Sprinkle over the hazelnuts, Parmesan, and lemon zest and cook for 2 minutes longer. Transfer to a serving bowl and squeeze over the lemon juice to serve.

Air
Fryer

Garlic Bread

YIELD:
4 servings
PREP TIME:
10 minutes
COOK TIME:
5 minutes

INGREDIENTS

3 tablespoons (42 g) unsalted butter, at room temperature
1 tablespoon (3 g) finely chopped chives (about 5)
1 large clove garlic, very finely chopped
¼ teaspoon kosher salt
⅛ teaspoon freshly ground black pepper
One 6- to 8-inch (15 to 20 cm) hoagie or submarine roll

1. In a small bowl, use a fork to mash together the butter, chives, garlic, salt, and pepper.

2. Slice the bread most, but not all the way through, in ¾-inch (2 cm)-thick increments. Generously spread the butter mixture in between the slices.

3. Lightly wrap the roll in aluminum foil and transfer to the Air Fryer rack. Cook at 390°F (200°C) until the bread is warm and crispy, 4 to 5 minutes.

Air
Fryer

Coconut Oil Roasted Potatoes

Air Fry

YIELD:
2 servings
PREP TIME:
5 minutes
COOK TIME:
15 minutes

INGREDIENTS

2 medium russet potatoes, peeled and cut into 1½-inch (3.8 cm) pieces
2 teaspoons coconut oil, melted
½ teaspoon kosher salt
¼ teaspoon freshly ground black pepper

1. In a large bowl, toss the potatoes with the coconut oil and season with the salt and pepper.

2. Transfer to the Air Fryer rack and shake into an even layer. Cook at 400°F (205°C) until tender and golden brown, removing the fryer basket to toss potatoes half way through Air Frying. Cook for about 15 minutes, or until desired level of crispiness.

Air
Fryer

Air Fry

YIELD:
4 servings
PREP TIME:
10 minutes
COOK TIME:
33 minutes

Veggie Chips

INGREDIENTS

- 1 medium small beet (about 4 ounces, or 112 g), peeled and very thinly sliced
- 6 teaspoons (30 ml) extra-virgin olive oil, divided
- Kosher salt and freshly ground black pepper
- 1 small sweet potato (about 4 ounces, or 112), peeled and very thinly sliced
- 1 carrot (about 4 ounces, or 112 g), peeled into long ribbons

1. In a large bowl, toss the beets with 2 teaspoons (10 ml) of the olive oil and season with a pinch each of salt and pepper. Transfer to the Air Fryer rack and cook at 330°F (165°C) until tender and starting to turn color, about 15 minutes, shaking the pan every few minutes. Transfer to a wire rack to cool.

2. Repeat with the sweet potato and 2 teaspoons (10 ml) oil, cooking until the potatoes are just starting to color, 8 to 10 minutes. Transfer to a wire rack to cool.

3. Repeat with the carrots and remaining 2 teaspoons (10 ml) oil, cooking until the carrots are just starting to color, about 8 minutes. Transfer to a wire rack to cool. The vegetables will continue to crisp as they cool.

BEEF
AND LAMB
MAINS

Instant Pot

Apple Cider and Thyme-Braised Brisket

YIELD:
6 servings
PREP TIME:
15 minutes
COOK TIME:
1 hour 10 minutes

INGREDIENTS

1 tablespoon (15 ml) extra-virgin olive oil
2½ pounds (1.1 kg) beef brisket
1½ teaspoons kosher salt
½ teaspoon freshly ground black pepper
6 cloves garlic, smashed
2 tablespoons (32 g) tomato paste
1 cup (235 ml) apple cider
2 tablespoons (30 ml) apple cider vinegar
1 tablespoon (20 g) honey
8 sprigs fresh thyme
3 tablespoons (12 g) chopped fresh flat-leaf parsley
3 tablespoons (12 g) chopped fresh dill

1. Turn the Instant Pot on to [Sauté]. Heat the olive oil. Season the brisket with the salt and pepper. Add to the pot and cook until browned, about 5 minutes per side. Transfer to a plate.

2. Add the garlic to the pot and cook, stirring, for 30 seconds. Add the tomato paste, apple cider, vinegar, honey, and thyme, and cook for 1 minute, stirring and scraping up any brown bits from the bottom of the pot. Press [Cancel].

3. Add the brisket to the pot. Lock the lid. Press [Manual] and cook on high pressure for 55 minutes. Use the "Quick Release" method to vent the steam, then open the lid.

4. Transfer the brisket to a cutting board and let rest for a few minutes. Press [Cancel], then press [Sauté]. Discard the thyme sprigs. Let the sauce thicken to the desired consistency.

5. Thinly slice the brisket against the grain and transfer to a platter. Spoon the sauce over the top and sprinkle with the parsley and dill.

Instant Pot

Sauté   Manual

Braised Lamb Souvlaki

YIELD:
4 servings
PREP TIME:
15 minutes
COOK TIME:
45 minutes

INGREDIENTS

1 lemon
1 tablespoon (2 g) finely chopped fresh rosemary
2 teaspoons paprika
2 teaspoons ground cumin
½ teaspoon ground coriander
¾ teaspoon kosher salt, divided
¾ teaspoon freshly ground black pepper, divided
1½ pounds (680 g) boneless leg of lamb, trimmed and cut into 3-inch (7.5 cm) pieces
2 tablespoons (30 ml) extra-virgin olive oil, divided
2 cloves garlic, finely chopped
1 cup (235 ml) less-sodium chicken broth
2 tablespoons (32 g) tomato paste
¼ small red onion, thinly sliced
2 plum tomatoes, cut into wedges
¼ cup (25 g) pitted Kalamata olives, halved
4 flatbreads, warmed
Plain yogurt, for serving (see page 16 for instructions on how to make yogurt)
¼ cup (37 g) crumbled feta cheese

1. Using a vegetable peeler, remove 3 strips of zest from the lemon and thinly slice crosswise. Set aside.

2. In a small bowl, combine the rosemary, paprika, cumin, coriander, ½ teaspoon of the salt, and ½ teaspoon of the pepper. Rub the mixture all over the lamb to coat.

3. Turn the Instant Pot on to [Sauté]. Heat 1 tablespoon (15 ml) of the olive oil. Add the lamb and cook until browned on all sides, about 5 minutes total. Add the garlic and cook, stirring, for 1 minute. Add the chicken broth, tomato paste, and lemon zest, and cook, stirring, for 1 minute. Press [Cancel]. Lock the lid.

4. Press [Manual] and cook on high pressure for 40 minutes. Use the "Quick Release" method to vent the steam, then open the lid. Using 2 forks, shred the lamb and toss it in the cooking liquid.

5. Twenty minutes before the lamb is finished, place the onion in a medium bowl. Squeeze the juice of half the lemon on top and toss to combine. Let sit for 5 minutes. Add the tomatoes, olives, and the remaining 1 tablespoon (15 ml) olive oil, ¼ teaspoon salt, and ¼ teaspoon pepper, and toss to combine.

6. Spread each flatbread with some yogurt, then top with the lamb and the tomato salad. Sprinkle the crumbled feta cheese on top before serving.

Instant Pot

Sauté   Manual

YIELD:
6 servings
PREP TIME:
15 minutes
COOK TIME:
15 minutes

Chili Dogs

INGREDIENTS

1 tablespoon (15 ml) extra-virgin olive oil
1 medium red onion, finely chopped, divided
8 ounces (225 g) lean ground beef
1 tablespoon (7.5 g) chili powder
2 teaspoons ground cumin
⅛ teaspoon ground cinnamon
1 can (14½ ounces, or 410 g) crushed tomatoes
2 tablespoons (22 g) yellow mustard
1 tablespoon (15 g) light brown sugar
1 teaspoon Worcestershire sauce
6 hot dogs
1 half-sour pickle, chopped, plus 2 tablespoons (30 ml) brine
2 tablespoons (8 g) chopped fresh flat-leaf parsley
6 hot dog buns
Shredded Cheddar cheese, for serving

1. Turn the Instant Pot on to [Sauté]. Heat the olive oil, add all but 2 tablespoons (20 g) of the onion, and cook, stirring occasionally, for 5 minutes. Add the beef and cook, breaking it up into small pieces until no longer pink, about 4 minutes. Stir in the chili powder, cumin, and cinnamon, and cook for 1 minute.

2. Add the tomatoes, mustard, brown sugar, and Worcestershire, and stir to combine. Press [Cancel]. Nestle the hot dogs in the chili. Lock the lid. Press [Manual] and cook on high pressure for 2 minutes. Use the "Quick Release" method to vent the steam, then open the lid.

3. Meanwhile, in a small bowl, combine the pickle, brine, parsley, and the reserved onion.

4. Nestle the hot dogs in buns and top with the chili and Cheddar. Serve with the pickle-onion relish.

Sauté   Manual

Chili-Garlic Beef with Quick-Pickled Cucumbers

YIELD:
4 servings
PREP TIME:
20 minutes
COOK TIME:
45 minutes

INGREDIENTS

2 tablespoons (30 ml) canola oil
2 pounds (907 g) chuck steak, trimmed and cut into 1½-inch (4 cm) pieces
1½ teaspoons five-spice powder
½ cup (120 ml) less-sodium soy sauce
¾ cup (180 ml) water
¼ cup (60 g) plus 1 tablespoon (15 g) packed light brown sugar, divided
1 tablespoon (8 g) plus 1 teaspoon finely grated fresh ginger, divided
2½ teaspoons chili-garlic sauce, divided
2 large cloves garlic, finely chopped
¼ cup (60 ml) rice vinegar
1 seedless cucumber, thinly sliced
¼ small sweet onion, thinly sliced
1 tablespoon (8 g) cornstarch
1 tablespoon (15 ml) water
White rice, for serving
1 tablespoon (8 g) toasted sesame seeds, for serving

1. Turn the Instant Pot on to [Sauté]. Heat the canola oil. Season the beef with the five-spice powder. Working in batches, cook the beef until browned on all sides, about 5 minutes. Transfer to a plate.

2. Meanwhile, in a small bowl, combine the soy sauce, water, ¼ cup (60 g) of the brown sugar, 1 tablespoon (8 g) of the ginger, and 2 teaspoons of the chili-garlic sauce. Stir until the sugar dissolves.

3. Add the garlic to the pot and cook, stirring, for 1 minute. Add the soy sauce mixture and cook, scraping up any bits on the bottom of the pot. Press [Cancel]. Return the beef to the pot and lock the lid. Press [Manual] and cook on high pressure for 30 minutes. Use the "Quick Release" method to vent the steam, then open the lid.

4. While the beef is cooking, make the cucumbers. In a medium bowl, whisk together the vinegar with the remaining 1 tablespoon (15 g) brown sugar, 1 teaspoon ginger, and ½ teaspoon chili-garlic sauce. Add the cucumber and onion, and toss to combine.

5. In a small bowl, combine the cornstarch with the water. Add to the pot, then turn the pot on to [Sauté] and simmer until slightly thickened, about 3 minutes. Serve the beef and sauce over the rice and top with the pickled cucumbers and sesame seeds.

Instant
Pot

or

(Sauté) (Slow Cook) | (Sauté) (Manual)

YIELD:
4 servings
PREP TIME:
25 minutes
COOK TIME:
8 hours 15 minutes
(slow cook)
55 minutes (pressure cook)

Beef Ragù

INGREDIENTS

2 tablespoons (30 ml) extra-virgin olive oil, divided, plus more if necessary
1½ pounds (680 g) chuck steak, trimmed and cut into 2-inch (5 cm) pieces
¾ teaspoon kosher salt
½ teaspoon freshly ground black pepper
1 large yellow onion, chopped
4 cloves garlic, finely chopped
2 tablespoons (32 g) tomato paste
2 medium carrots, cut into ¼-inch (6 mm) pieces
1 rib celery, cut into ¼-inch (6 mm) pieces
1 cup (235 ml) dry red wine, such as Cabernet Sauvignon
1 can (28 ounces, or 795 g) whole peeled tomatoes, drained and crushed with your hands
2 anchovy fillets, chopped
2 sprigs fresh rosemary
2 sprigs fresh sage
12 ounces (340 g) pappardelle or other wide pasta
Grated Parmesan cheese, for serving

1. Turn the Instant Pot on to [Sauté]. Heat 1 tablespoon (15 ml) of the olive oil. Season the beef with the salt and pepper. Add half the beef to the pot and cook until browned, about 5 minutes total. Transfer to a plate. Repeat with the remaining beef, adding more olive oil to the pot, if necessary.

2. Add the remaining 1 tablespoon (15 ml) olive oil and the onion, and cook, stirring occasionally, for 3 minutes. Add the garlic and cook, stirring, for 1 minute. Stir in the tomato paste and cook for 1 minute.

3. Add the carrots, celery, and wine, and cook, scraping up any brown bits, for 1 minute. Add the tomatoes followed by the anchovies, rosemary, and sage. Return the meat to the pot. Press [Cancel]. Lock the lid.

4. In this step, you have the option to slow-cook or pressure-cook (don't do both!). To slow-cook: Press [Slow Cook], leave the vent open, and cook on "More" for 8 hours. To pressure-cook: Press [Manual] and cook on high pressure for 40 minutes. Use the "Quick Release" method to vent the steam, then open the lid.

5. Twenty minutes before serving, cook the pasta according to the package directions.

6. Open the lid and discard the rosemary and sage. Press [Cancel], then press [Sauté] and simmer until the sauce is slightly thickened, about 5 minutes.

7. Using 2 forks, break the meat into slightly smaller pieces. Toss the ragù with the pasta and serve sprinkled with Parmesan.

Instant Pot

Mediterranean Stuffed Tomatoes

YIELD:
4 servings
PREP TIME:
15 minutes
COOK TIME:
20 minutes

INGREDIENTS

1 lemon
2 tablespoons (30 ml) extra-
    virgin olive oil
1 small yellow onion,
    finely chopped
2 cloves garlic, finely chopped
1 tablespoon (2 g) fresh
    thyme leaves
12 ounces (340 g) lean
    ground beef
¾ teaspoon kosher salt, divided
½ teaspoon freshly ground black
    pepper, divided
½ cup (120 ml) dry white wine,
    such as Pinot Grigio
2 tablespoons (8 g) chopped
    fresh flat-leaf parsley
2 ounces (55 g) feta cheese,
    crumbled
4 large beefsteak tomatoes
Mixed green salad, for serving

1. Finely grate the zest of the lemon. Turn the Instant Pot on to [Sauté]. Heat the olive oil. Add the onion and cook, stirring often, until tender and beginning to turn golden brown, 8 to 10 minutes. Stir in the garlic and thyme, and cook for 1 minute.

2. Add the beef, ½ teaspoon of the salt, and ¼ teaspoon of the pepper, and cook, breaking up the meat with a spoon, until browned, 6 to 8 minutes. Add the wine and simmer for 2 minutes. Press [Cancel]. Transfer the beef to a bowl and squeeze the juice of the lemon over the top. Add the lemon zest, parsley, and feta, and gently toss to combine.

3. Wipe out the pot, then insert the steam rack and add ½ cup (120 ml) water.

4. Using a sharp knife and working on an angle, remove the tomato stem from each tomato, leaving a 2-inch-wide (5 cm) opening in the tomatoes. With a spoon, scoop out most of the seeds and pulp (without breaking the skin). Season the inside of the tomatoes with the remaining ¼ teaspoon salt and ¼ teaspoon pepper. Divide the meat mixture among the tomatoes (about a heaping ½ cup, or 113 g, each).

5. Place the tomatoes on the rack. Lock the lid. Press [Manual] and cook on high pressure for 1 minute. Use the "Quick Release" method to vent the steam, then open the lid. Serve the stuffed tomatoes with a mixed green salad.

Instant Pot

Balsamic Beef Short Ribs

YIELD:
4 servings
PREP TIME:
20 minutes
COOK TIME:
1 hour

INGREDIENTS

1 tablespoon (15 ml) extra-virgin olive oil
8 bone-in beef short ribs (about 3½ pounds, or 1.6 kg)
1½ teaspoons kosher salt
½ teaspoon freshly ground black pepper
6 cloves garlic, smashed
1 can (14½ ounces, or 410 g) crushed tomatoes
½ cup (120 ml) balsamic vinegar
½ cup (120 ml) water
8 sprigs fresh thyme
2 bay leaves
1 medium yellow onion, quartered
1¼ pounds (570 g) whole baby potatoes (about 16)
3 tablespoons (12 g) chopped fresh flat-leaf parsley
1 teaspoon finely grated lemon zest

1. Turn the Instant Pot on to [Sauté]. Heat the olive oil. Season the short ribs with the salt and pepper. Add half of the ribs to the pot and cook until browned, about 3 minutes per side. Transfer to a plate. Repeat with the remaining short ribs.

2. Add the garlic to the pot and cook, stirring, for 30 seconds. Add the tomatoes, vinegar, water, thyme, and bay leaves.

3. Nestle the short ribs and onion into the sauce and place the potatoes on top. Press [Cancel]. Lock the lid. Press [Manual] and cook on high pressure for 45 minutes. Use the "Quick Release" method to vent the steam, then open the lid.

4. Divide the potatoes among plates and smash them with the back of a fork. Place the short ribs and onions on top of the potatoes. Discard the bay leaves and thyme sprigs. Spoon some of the sauce over the short ribs and sprinkle with the parsley and lemon zest.

Marinated Beef, Pepper, and Onion Kebabs

YIELD:
8 kebabs
PREP TIME:
20 minutes, plus 2 hours to marinate
COOK TIME:
8 minutes

INGREDIENTS

MARINADE
1 tablespoon (15 ml) extra-virgin olive oil
2 tablespoons (30 ml) low-sodium soy sauce
2 teaspoons fresh lemon juice
2 teaspoons red wine vinegar
1 teaspoon Dijon mustard
1 teaspoon honey
1 clove garlic, very finely chopped
½ teaspoon freshly ground black pepper

KEBABS
1 pound (454 g) top sirloin, cut into 1-inch (2.5 cm) cubes
1 red onion, cut into 1-inch (2.5 cm) chunks
1 green bell pepper, cored, seeded, and cut into 1-inch (2.5 cm) chunks

1. To make the marinade: In a large zip-top bag, place the olive oil, soy sauce, lemon juice, red wine vinegar, mustard, honey, garlic and black pepper. Massage the ingredients together to combine.

2. To make the kebabs: Add the cubed sirloin to the marinade and massage the outside of the bag to coat in the mixture. Refrigerate for at least 2 hours or up to 24 hours. Once ready to cook, thread the steak, alternating with the onion and pepper, onto eight 6-inch (15 cm) bamboo skewers.

3. Transfer to the Air Fryer rack and cook at 380°F (195°C) until lightly charred and cooked to your desired doneness, 6 to 8 minutes.

Air Fryer

Stuffed Peppers

Air Fry

YIELD:
2 servings
PREP TIME:
15 minutes
COOK TIME:
35 minutes

INGREDIENTS

2 red, yellow, or orange bell
peppers
1 tablespoon (15 ml) extra-virgin
olive oil
1 small onion, finely chopped
3 ounces (84 g) (1 small) zucchini
or summer squash, cut into
¼-inch (6 mm) pieces
2 ounces (56 g) (about 4) button
mushrooms, chopped
2 cloves garlic, chopped
½ teaspoon dried oregano
1 tablespoon (15 g) tomato paste
6 ounces (168 g) 90% lean
ground beef
½ teaspoon kosher salt
¼ teaspoon freshly ground black
pepper
1 cup (240 ml) marinara sauce
½ cup (80 g) cooked rice
2 ounces (56 g) extra-sharp
Cheddar cheese, grated,
divided

1. Cut the tops off of the peppers, discard the seeds, and chop the core.

2. Heat the oil in a large skillet over medium heat. Add the onion, zucchini, mushrooms, and chopped pepper cores and cook, stirring occasionally, until softened and starting to turn golden, about 10 minutes.

3. Add the garlic and cook, stirring, for 1 minute. Add the oregano and tomato paste and cook, stirring, for 1 minute. Add the beef, salt, and pepper, and cook, breaking up the beef with the back of a spoon, until brown, 2 to 3 minutes. Add the marinara sauce, rice, and half of the cheese, stirring to coat. Remove from the heat.

4. Fill the peppers with the mixture (about 1 cup, or 240 g, per pepper) and transfer to the Air Fryer rack. Cook at 360°F (185°C) for 15 minutes. Top with the remaining cheese and cook until the cheese has melted, about 2 minutes more.

Beef Taquitos

YIELD:
4 servings
PREP TIME:
20 minutes
COOK TIME:
10 minutes

INGREDIENTS

2 teaspoons extra-virgin olive oil,
   plus more for brushing
8 ounces (227 g) 90% lean
   ground beef
1 clove garlic, finely chopped
½ teaspoon ground cumin
½ teaspoon ground coriander
½ teaspoon dried oregano
1 teaspoon chili powder
¼ teaspoon kosher salt
1 tablespoon (15 g) tomato paste
¼ cup (60 ml) water
2 ounces (56 g) cream cheese
Four 6-inch (15 cm) thin corn or
   flour tortillas
Sour cream, shredded cheese,
   sliced avocado, and salsa,
   for serving

1. Heat the oil in a large nonstick skillet over medium-high heat. Add the beef and cook, stirring and breaking up the meat with the back of a spoon, until brown throughout and starting to turn dark brown at the edges, 3 to 4 minutes.

2. Add the garlic, cumin, coriander, oregano, chili powder, and salt and cook, stirring, for 1 minute. Add the tomato paste and stir to combine. Add the water, stirring to coat and slightly loosen the mixture. Remove the pan from the heat and add cream cheese to melt.

3. Wrap tortillas in a damp paper towel and microwave for 3 seconds to soften. Divide the mixture among the tortillas, placing it in the center in a rectangular shape. Roll up the tortillas and place them seam-side down on the Air Fryer rack. Brush the outsides with oil.

4. Cook at 380°F (195°C) until crisp and golden brown, 4 to 5 minutes. Serve with sour cream, shredded cheese, avocado, and salsa.

Feta-Stuffed Kibbeh

Air Fry

YIELD:
10 to 12 balls

PREP TIME:
10 minutes, plus
40 minutes to chill

COOK TIME:
20 minutes

INGREDIENTS

DOUGH
½ cup (60 g) bulgur wheat
¼ teaspoon kosher salt
1 small onion, roughly chopped
8 ounces (227 g) finely ground
   lean lamb or beef
¼ teaspoon ground cinnamon
¼ teaspoon ground allspice
¼ teaspoon ground chili powder

FILLING
1 tablespoon (15 ml) extra-virgin
   olive oil
1 small onion, finely chopped
3 tablespoons (24 g) toasted
   pine nuts
¼ cup (38 g) crumbled feta
   cheese
¼ cup (16 g) finely chopped fresh
   flat-leaf parsley

Labne, hummus, and pita bread,
   for serving

1. To make the dough: Place the bulgur wheat in a medium bowl and cover with cold water and the salt. Let sit for 20 minutes. Drain through a fine-mesh sieve, then squeeze dry using a kitchen towel or cheesecloth.

2. Transfer to a food processor along with the onion and pulse until finely chopped. Transfer to a bowl and add the meat, cinnamon, allspice, and chili powder; use your hands to mix into a paste. Refrigerate for 20 minutes.

3. To make the filling: Heat the oil in a large skillet over medium heat and cook the onion, stirring occasionally, until tender and starting to turn golden, 8 to 10 minutes. Transfer to a bowl and add the pine nuts, feta cheese, and parsley.

4. Shape the kibbeh. Form the paste into golf ball–size balls; you should get 10 to 12. Holding one ball in your hand, make an indentation with your thumb and work it into a thin, hollow shell. Add 1½ teaspoons of the filling into the indent, and then pinch the filling inside and shape the ball into a football shape. Transfer to a baking sheet and repeat with the remaining dough and filling.

5. Transfer half of the kibbeh to the Air Fryer rack and cook at 360°F (185°C) until golden brown and cooked through, 8 to 10 minutes. Repeat with the remaining kibbeh. Serve with labne, hummus, and pita bread.

POULTRY MAINS

Instant
Pot

Enchiladas Rancheras

YIELD:
6 servings
PREP TIME:
30 minutes
COOK TIME:
35 minutes

INGREDIENTS

1 tablespoon (15 ml) plus ⅓ cup (80 ml) canola oil, divided
½ medium white onion, chopped
2 cloves garlic, smashed
2 pounds (907 g) beefsteak tomatoes, quartered and cored
1 serrano chile, seeded
2 ancho chiles, seeded
1¼ teaspoons kosher salt
¼ cup (60 ml) water
4 bone-in chicken breasts (about 3 pounds, or 1.4 kg)
12 corn tortillas

FOR SERVING
Crumbled queso fresco
Sliced avocado
Sliced red onion
Fresh sprigs cilantro

1   Turn the Instant Pot on to [Sauté]. Heat 1 tablespoon (15 ml) of the canola oil. Add the onion and garlic, and cook, stirring often, for 2 minutes. Add the tomatoes, serrano chile, ancho chiles, salt, and water, and stir to combine. Place the chicken breasts on top of the tomato mixture. Press [Cancel].

2. Lock the lid. Press [Manual] and cook on high pressure for 15 minutes. Use the "Quick Release" method to vent the steam, then open the lid. Transfer the chicken to a bowl and, when cool enough to handle, shred the meat, discarding the skin and bones.

3. Meanwhile, fry the tortillas: Heat the remaining ⅓ cup (80 ml) canola oil in a small skillet over medium heat. Working with 1 tortilla at a time, cook for 15 seconds per side, then transfer to a paper towel–lined plate.

4. Using a handheld immersion blender (or a regular blender), purée the tomato mixture. Press [Sauté] and simmer the sauce until it thickens to the desired consistency (or until it reduces to about 3½ cups, or 825 ml). Spoon ½ cup (120 ml) of the sauce into the chicken in the bowl and toss to combine.

5. Preheat oven to 375°F (190°C, or gas mark 5).

6. Spread a thin layer of sauce over the bottom of a 13 x 9-inch (33 x 23 cm) baking dish. Dividing evenly, roll the chicken up in the tortillas and place seam side down in the baking dish. Smother with the remaining sauce. Bake until the sauce bubbles, 10 to 15 minutes.

7. Serve the enchiladas topped with cheese, avocado, onion, and cilantro.

Instant
Pot

Lemon Chicken with Green Olives

YIELD:
4 servings
PREP TIME:
15 minutes
COOK TIME:
30 minutes

INGREDIENTS

- 1 tablespoon (15 ml) extra-virgin olive oil
- 8 bone-in, skin-on chicken thighs (about 3 pounds, or 1.4 kg)
- ¾ teaspoon kosher salt
- ½ teaspoon freshly ground black pepper
- 4 cloves garlic, thinly sliced
- 1 medium yellow onion, thinly sliced
- 1 lemon, sliced into thin rounds
- 1 cup (100 g) pitted green olives
- 6 sprigs fresh thyme
- 2 tablespoons (8 g) chopped fresh flat-leaf parsley

1. Turn the Instant Pot on to [Sauté]. Heat the olive oil. Pat the chicken dry with paper towels and season with the salt and pepper. Add half of the chicken, skin side down, and cook until the skin is golden brown and crisp, about 10 minutes. Flip the chicken and cook for 1 minute more. Transfer to a plate and repeat with the remaining chicken.

2. Add the garlic to the pot and cook, stirring, for 30 seconds. Add the onion, lemon, olives, and thyme, and cook, scraping up the brown bits from the bottom of the pot, for 2 minutes. Lay the chicken on top. Press [Cancel].

3. Lock the lid. Press [Manual] and cook on high pressure for 10 minutes. Use the "Quick Release" method to vent the steam, then open the lid.

4. Serve the chicken with the onions, lemons, and olives, and sprinkle with the parsley.

Instant Pot

Colombian Chicken Soup

YIELD:
4 servings
PREP TIME:
10 minutes
COOK TIME:
20 minutes

INGREDIENTS

- 1 medium yellow onion, cut in half
- 2 medium carrots, cut in half crosswise
- 2 ribs celery, cut in half crosswise
- 3 bone-in chicken breasts (about 2 pounds, or 907 g)
- 5 cups (1.2 L) water
- 1½ teaspoons kosher salt
- 1½ pounds (680 g) Yukon gold potatoes, cut into ½-inch (13 mm) pieces
- 1 ear corn, cut into 4 pieces
- ¼ teaspoon freshly ground black pepper
- 1 avocado
- ¼ cup (60 g) sour cream
- 1 tablespoon (9 g) capers, rinsed
- 1 teaspoon dried oregano
- 8 sprigs fresh cilantro
- 1 lime, quartered

1. To the Instant Pot, add the onion, carrots, celery, chicken, water, and salt. Lock the lid. Press [Manual] and cook on high pressure for 15 minutes. Use the "Quick Release" method to vent the steam, then open the lid. Transfer the chicken to a large bowl. When cool enough to handle, shred into pieces, discarding the skin and bones.

2. Discard the onion, carrots, and celery. Add the potatoes and corn to the broth. Lock the lid. Press [Manual] and cook on high pressure for 2 minutes. Use the "Quick Release" method to vent the steam, then open the lid. Stir in the chicken and pepper.

3. Divide the soup among bowls. Peel, pit, and slice the avocado. Top the soup with the avocado, sour cream, capers, oregano, and cilantro. Serve with the lime quarters for squeezing.

Instant Pot

Sauté   Manual

Hunter-Style Chicken

YIELD:
4 servings
PREP TIME:
25 minutes
COOK TIME:
25 minutes

INGREDIENTS

3 tablespoons (45 ml)
  extra-virgin olive oil, divided,
  plus more if necessary
10 ounces (280 g) cremini
  mushrooms, trimmed
  and quartered
4 bone-in chicken breasts,
  halved crosswise (about
  3 pounds, or 1.4 kg)
¾ teaspoon kosher salt
½ teaspoon freshly ground
  black pepper
1 medium yellow onion, chopped
4 cloves garlic, finely chopped
1 large carrot, peeled and sliced
  ¼ inch (6 mm) thick
½ cup (120 ml) dry red wine, such
  as Cabernet Sauvignon
8 sprigs fresh thyme
1 can (28 ounces, or 795 g)
  whole peeled tomatoes,
  drained
Chopped fresh flat-leaf parsley,
  for serving
Crusty bread, for serving

1. Turn the Instant Pot on to [Sauté]. Heat 1 tablespoon (15 ml) of the olive oil. Add the mushrooms and cook, stirring occasionally, until beginning to brown, about 4 minutes. Transfer to a plate.

2. Heat 1 tablespoon (15 ml) of the olive oil. Pat the chicken dry with paper towels and season with the salt and pepper. Add half the chicken, skin side down, and cook until the skin is golden brown and crisp, 4 to 6 minutes. Flip and cook for 1 minute more. Transfer to a plate. Repeat with the remaining chicken, adding more olive oil to the pot, if necessary.

3. Add the remaining 1 tablespoon (15 ml) olive oil and the onion, and cook, stirring occasionally, for 3 minutes. Add the garlic and cook, stirring, for 1 minute.

4. Add the carrot and wine, and cook, stirring and scraping up any brown bits on the bottom of the pot, for 1 minute. Add the thyme and tomatoes, crushing them with your hands as you add them to the pot. Add the mushrooms and mix to combine. Press [Cancel].

5. Arrange the chicken on top of the tomato mixture. Lock the lid. Press [Manual] and cook on high pressure for 10 minutes. Use the "Quick Release" method to vent the steam, then open the lid.

6. Serve the chicken and vegetables sprinkled with parsley and crusty bread alongside.

Instant Pot

Sauté   Manual

Chicken Marbella

YIELD:
4 servings
PREP TIME:
15 minutes
COOK TIME:
25 minutes

INGREDIENTS

8 bone-in, skin-on chicken thighs (about 3 pounds, or 1.4 kg)
1 teaspoon dried oregano
¾ teaspoon kosher salt
½ teaspoon freshly ground black pepper
1 tablespoon (15 ml) extra-virgin olive oil, plus more if necessary
3 tablespoons (45 ml) red wine vinegar
2 tablespoons (30 g) packed light brown sugar
1 tablespoon (9 g) capers, plus 1 tablespoon (15 ml) brine
4 cloves garlic, thinly sliced
½ cup (120 ml) dry white wine, such as Pinot Grigio
¾ cup (131 g) pitted prunes, halved
½ cup (50 g) pitted green olives
Chopped fresh flat-leaf parsley, for serving

1. Turn the Instant Pot on to [Sauté]. Pat the chicken dry with paper towels and season with the oregano, salt, and pepper.

2. Heat the olive oil. Add half of the chicken, skin side down, and cook until the skin is golden brown and crisp, 8 to 10 minutes. Flip and cook for 1 minute more. Transfer to a plate and repeat with the remaining chicken (adding more olive oil to the pot if necessary).

3. Meanwhile, in a small bowl, whisk together the vinegar, brown sugar, and caper brine.

4. Add the garlic to the pot and cook, stirring, for 30 seconds. Add the wine and cook, stirring and scraping up any brown bits, for 1 minute. Add the vinegar mixture along with the prunes, olives, and capers. Press [Cancel].

5. Nestle the chicken in the olive mixture. Lock the lid. Press [Manual] and cook on high pressure for 10 minutes. Use the "Quick Release" method to vent the steam, then open the lid.

6. Serve the chicken with the olives, prunes, and a bit of the juices, and sprinkle with parsley.

Instant
Pot

Sauté Manual

Cranberry and Herb-Stuffed Turkey Breast

YIELD:
4 to 6 servings
PREP TIME:
25 minutes
COOK TIME:
45 minutes

INGREDIENTS

¼ cup (30 g) dried bread crumbs

¼ cup (15 g) chopped fresh flat-leaf parsley

2 tablespoons (5 g) chopped fresh sage

2 teaspoons chopped fresh rosemary

2 cloves garlic, finely chopped

½ cup (60 g) dried cranberries, finely chopped

1½ teaspoons kosher salt, divided

¾ teaspoon freshly ground black pepper, divided

¼ cup (60 ml) extra-virgin olive oil, divided

1 boneless turkey breast (3 pounds, or 1.4 kg)

1 teaspoon paprika

¼ cup (60 ml) dry white wine, such as Pinot Grigio

1. In a small bowl, combine the bread crumbs, parsley, sage, rosemary, garlic, cranberries, ¼ teaspoon of the salt, ⅛ teaspoon of the pepper, and 3 tablespoons (45 ml) of the olive oil. Stir well to combine.

2. Butterfly the turkey breast: Place the breast on a cutting board, skin side down. Using a chef's knife, hold the blade parallel to the board and slice into the breast, starting at the thickest part. Cut along the length of the breast but not all the way through. Open it up like a book.

3. Season the inside with ¼ teaspoon of the salt and ⅛ teaspoon of the pepper. Spoon the stuffing onto the center of the breast, spreading evenly from top to bottom. Starting with one long side, roll the breast into a log so the stuffing is tightly enclosed. Use 5 lengths of butcher's twine to tie up the breast at 2-inch (5 cm) intervals along the length of the breast. Season the outside with the paprika and the remaining 1 teaspoon salt and ½ teaspoon pepper.

4. Turn the Instant Pot on to [Sauté]. Heat the remaining 1 tablespoon (15 ml) olive oil. Add the turkey and cook until all sides are golden brown, 10 to 12 minutes. Add the wine. Press [Cancel].

5. Lock the lid. Press [Manual] and cook on high pressure for 30 minutes. Use the "Quick Release" method to vent the steam, then open the lid. Transfer the turkey to a cutting board and let rest for 5 minutes before slicing.

Air Fry

Creamy Chicken and Mushroom Pies

YIELD:
4 servings
PREP TIME:
30 minutes
COOK TIME:
20 minutes

INGREDIENTS

- 1 tablespoon (15 ml) extra-virgin olive oil
- 6 ounces (168 g) sliced cremini mushrooms
- ½ teaspoon kosher salt
- ¼ teaspoon freshly ground black pepper
- 4 ounces (112 g) cream cheese, at room temperature
- 5 ounces (140 g) shredded rotisserie chicken (about 1 cup, or 140 g)
- 1 tablespoon (11 g) Dijon mustard
- 1 tablespoon (15 ml) fresh lemon juice
- ¼ cup (15 g) roughly chopped fresh flat-leaf parsley
- All-purpose flour, for dusting
- 1 prepared puff pastry sheet (about 8 ounces, or 227 g)
- 1 large egg, lightly beaten

1. Heat the oil in a large skillet over medium-high heat. Add the mushrooms, salt, and pepper and cook, tossing occasionally, until starting to soften and turn golden, 2 to 3 minutes. Remove from the heat and add the cream cheese, stirring to melt.

2. Fold in the chicken, mustard, lemon juice, and parsley. Let cool to room temperature.

3. Lightly flour a work surface and roll the pastry into an 11-inch (28 cm) square. Cut the pastry in half. Divide the chicken and mushroom mixture in half and place each portion on one end of each rectangle of pastry, leaving a ½-inch (1.3 cm) border on all sides.

4. Brush the border with the egg and fold over the other half of the puff pastry. Use a fork to crimp and seal the edges. Brush the tops lightly with the egg mixture.

5. Transfer 2 of the pies to the Air Fryer rack and cook at 370°F (190°C) for 6 minutes. Turn the pies over and continue cooking until golden brown on all sides, 3 to 4 minutes longer. Repeat with the remaining pies.

YIELD:
4 servings
PREP TIME:
15 minutes
COOK TIME:
15 minutes, plus
cook time for rice

Chicken Fajitas

INGREDIENTS

CHICKEN
½ cup (85 g) rice
1 tablespoon (15 ml) extra-virgin olive oil
2 teaspoons chili powder
½ teaspoon kosher salt
1 teaspoon coriander seeds, roughly crushed in mortar and pestle or spice grinder
8 ounces (227 g) chicken breast, cut into ¼-inch (6 mm)-thick slices
2 bell peppers, cored, seeded, and cut into ½-inch (1.3 cm)-thick strips
1 small red onion, cut into ½-inch (1.3 cm) wedges
1 tablespoon (15 ml) fresh lime juice

SAUCE
¼ cup (60 g) sour cream
¼ cup (4 g) chopped fresh cilantro
1 tablespoon (15 ml) fresh lime juice

1. To make the chicken: Cook the rice according to package directions.

2. In a large bowl, combine the olive oil, chili powder, salt, and coriander. Add the chicken, bell peppers, and onion and toss to coat evenly.

3. Line the Air Fryer rack with foil and place the chicken, peppers, and onion wedges on top. Cook at 350°F (180°C) until the chicken is cooked through and the vegetables are tender, about 15 minutes. Squeeze over the lime juice.

4. To make the sauce: Meanwhile, in a small food processor, pulse the sour cream, cilantro, and lime juice until almost completely smooth.

5. Serve the chicken with the rice and spoon over the sauce.

Pastrami-Spiced Chicken

YIELD:
2 servings
PREP TIME:
10 minutes
COOK TIME:
20 minutes

INGREDIENTS

1 tablespoon (5 g) coriander
   seeds
2 teaspoons black peppercorns
½ teaspoon fennel seeds
½ teaspoon yellow mustard seeds
2 teaspoons extra-virgin olive oil
1 teaspoon brown sugar
½ teaspoon paprika
½ teaspoon garlic powder
¼ teaspoon kosher salt
2 skin-on, boneless
   chicken breasts

1. In a spice grinder or mortar and pestle, coarsely grind the coriander seeds, peppercorns, fennel seeds, and mustard seeds. Transfer to a small bowl and add the olive oil, brown sugar, paprika, garlic powder, and salt.

2. Rub the chicken breasts on all sides with the spice rub. Transfer the chicken to the Air Fryer rack, skin-side down, and cook at 350°F (180°C) for 15 minutes.

3. Flip the chicken, increase the heat to 380°F (195°C), and cook until the chicken registers 165°F (74°C) on a meat thermometer and the skin is crisp, about 5 minutes more.

Quinoa Chicken Nuggets

YIELD:
2 servings
PREP TIME:
20 minutes
COOK TIME:
10 minutes

INGREDIENTS

⅓ cup (40 g) all-purpose flour
½ teaspoon kosher salt
¼ teaspoon freshly ground
   black pepper
¼ teaspoon dried oregano
1 large egg
1¾ cups (325 g) cooked quinoa
   (from 1 cup, or 175 g, raw)
½ cup (50 g) grated Parmesan
1 pound (454 g) boneless,
   skinless chicken breasts, cut
   into 2-inch (5 cm) pieces

1. In a shallow bowl or pie dish, whisk together the flour, salt, pepper, and oregano. In a second shallow bowl or pie dish, lightly beat the egg. In a third shallow bowl or pie dish, combine the cooked quinoa and Parmesan.

2. Working with one piece at a time, coat the chicken in the flour, then coat in the egg, tapping off the excess. Transfer to the bowl with the quinoa and generously coat.

3. Transfer the chicken to the Air Fryer rack and cook at 390°F (200°C) until the quinoa is golden and the chicken registers 165°F (74°C) on a meat thermometer, 8 to 10 minutes.

Air Fry

YIELD:
2 servings
PREP TIME:
35 minutes
COOK TIME:
20 minutes

Chicken Kiev

INGREDIENTS

2 tablespoons (28 g) unsalted
  butter, softened
1 small clove garlic, finely grated
  (½ teaspoon)
¼ cup (25 g) freshly grated
  Parmesan cheese
2 tablespoons (8 g) finely
  chopped fresh parsley
½ teaspoon finely grated
  lemon zest
¼ teaspoon kosher salt, divided
¼ teaspoon freshly ground black
  pepper, divided
2 boneless, skinless chicken
  breasts
3 tablespoons (24 g) all-purpose
  flour
1 large egg
½ cup (60 g) panko bread crumbs
2 teaspoons extra-virgin olive oil

1. In a small bowl, use a fork to mash the butter, garlic, Parmesan, parsley, lemon zest, ⅛ teaspoon of the salt, and ⅛ teaspoon of the pepper. Using parchment paper, roll two even ½-inch (1.3 cm)-thick logs of butter and freeze until very firm, at least 20 minutes.

2. Insert a thin, sharp knife into the thickest part of each chicken breast and push it three-fourths of the way down to the thin end, being careful not to pierce through the outside of the breast. Move the knife from side to side to form a wide pocket with a narrow opening. Stuff the breasts with the butter mixture.

3. In a shallow bowl or pie dish, whisk together the flour, remaining ⅛ teaspoon salt, and remaining ⅛ teaspoon pepper. In a second shallow bowl or pie dish lightly beat the egg. In a third shallow bowl or pie dish, combine the panko with the oil.

4. Working with one piece at a time, coat the chicken in the flour, then coat in the egg, tapping off the excess. Transfer to the bowl with the panko and generously coat.

5. Transfer the chicken to the Air Fryer rack and cook at 350°F (180°C) for 15 minutes.

6. Flip the chicken, increase the heat to 380°F (195°C), and cook until the chicken registers 165°F (74°C) on a meat thermometer and the coating is crisp and golden, about 5 minutes more.

PORK
MAINS

Instant Pot

Sauté Slow Cook

or

Sauté Manual

Pulled Pork Sandwiches

YIELD:
4 servings
PREP TIME:
20 minutes
COOK TIME:
8 hours 20 minutes (slow cook), 1 hour 5 minutes (pressure cook)

INGREDIENTS

SPICE RUB
1 tablespoon (15 g) packed dark brown sugar
2 teaspoons chili powder
2 teaspoons ground cumin
1 teaspoon kosher salt
¼ teaspoon ground cinnamon
¼ teaspoon cayenne pepper
2 pounds (907 g) pork shoulder, cut into 3-inch (7.5 cm) pieces

SAUCE
1 cup (240 g) ketchup
¼ cup (85 g) unsulfured molasses
½ cup (120 ml) water
¼ cup (60 ml) apple cider vinegar
2 tablespoons (30 g) packed dark brown sugar
1 tablespoon (7.5 g) chili powder
1 tablespoon (11 g) Dijon mustard
2 teaspoons Worcestershire sauce
⅛ teaspoon cayenne pepper
1 tablespoon (15 ml) extra-virgin olive oil
1 medium yellow onion, thinly sliced
2 cloves garlic, finely chopped

SANDWICHES
4 rolls or buns, split
Your favorite coleslaw

1. To make the spice rub, in a small bowl, combine the brown sugar, chili powder, cumin, salt, cinnamon, and cayenne. Season the pork with the rub.

2. To make the sauce, in a medium bowl, whisk together the ketchup, molasses, water, vinegar, brown sugar, chili powder, mustard, Worcestershire, and cayenne.

3. Turn the Instant pot on to [Sauté]. Heat the olive oil. Add the onion and cook, stirring occasionally, for 3 minutes. Stir in the garlic and cook for 1 minute. Add the sauce and mix to combine. Press [Cancel].

4. Add the pork to the sauce and turn to coat. Lock the lid. Here you have the option to slow-cook or pressure-cook (don't do both!). To slow-cook: Press [Slow Cook], leave the vent open, and cook on "More" for 8 hours. To pressure-cook: Press [Manual] and cook on high pressure for 45 minutes. Use the "Quick Release" method to vent the steam, then open the lid.

5. Transfer the pork to a bowl. Press [Cancel], then press [Sauté] and simmer the sauce, stirring occasionally, until thickened, 3 to 5 minutes. Press [Cancel].

6. Using 2 forks, shred the pork, then return it to the pot and toss to coat. Pile the pork and coleslaw on the bottom halves of the buns and sandwich with the tops.

94   *Air Fryer Instant Pot Cookbook*

Instant Pot

Italian Sausage Meatballs

YIELD:
4 servings
PREP TIME:
20 minutes
COOK TIME:
25 minutes

INGREDIENTS

1 tablespoon (15 ml) extra-virgin olive oil

1 medium onion, finely chopped

1 large egg

2 tablespoons (30 ml) water

½ teaspoon kosher salt, divided

½ teaspoon freshly ground black pepper, divided

½ cup (60 g) panko bread crumbs

½ cup (50 g) grated Parmesan cheese, plus more for serving

¼ cup (15 g) chopped fresh flat-leaf parsley

3 cloves garlic, finely chopped

12 ounces (340 g) lean ground beef

8 ounces (225 g) sweet Italian sausage, casings removed

1 teaspoon dried oregano

2 tablespoons (32 g) tomato paste

1 can (28 ounces, or 795 g) crushed tomatoes

4 sprigs fresh basil, plus leaves for serving

FOR SERVING

4 slices country bread, toasted

Ricotta cheese

Mixed green salad

1. Turn the Instant Pot on to [Sauté]. Heat the olive oil. Add the onion and cook, stirring occasionally, until beginning to soften, 5 to 6 minutes.

2. While the onions are cooking, in a large bowl, beat the egg with the water, ¼ teaspoon of the salt, and ¼ teaspoon of the pepper; stir in the bread crumbs. Add the Parmesan, parsley, and one-third of the garlic, and mix to combine. Add the beef and sausage, and mix until everything is fully incorporated. Shape the mixture into 25 balls (about 1½ inches, or 4 cm, in diameter each).

3. Stir the oregano and the remaining two-thirds garlic, ¼ teaspoon salt, and ¼ teaspoon pepper into the onions, and cook for 1 minute. Add the tomato paste and cook, stirring, for 1 minute. Add the tomatoes and basil sprigs to the pot, and stir to combine. Press [Cancel].

4. Place the meatballs on top of the sauce. Lock the lid. Press [Manual] and cook on high pressure for 7 minutes. Use the "Natural Release" method for 10 minutes, then vent any remaining steam and open the lid.

5. Meanwhile, spread the toasted bread with ricotta and divide among plates.

6. Spoon the meatballs and sauce over the bread and sprinkle with additional Parmesan and fresh basil leaves. Serve with a green salad.

Instant Pot

Sauté   Manual

Hoppin' John Stew

YIELD:
4 servings
PREP TIME:
20 minutes
COOK TIME:
30 minutes

INGREDIENTS

2 tablespoons (30 ml) extra-virgin olive oil, divided
14 ounces (395 g) kielbasa, sliced into ½-inch-thick (13 mm) pieces
1 large yellow onion, chopped
4 cloves garlic, finely chopped
1½ cups (325 g) dried black-eyed peas, rinsed
3 cups (700 ml) less-sodium chicken broth
1 jalapeño, sliced
4 scallions (white and light green parts), thinly sliced
4 cups (120 g) baby spinach

FOR SERVING
White rice
Hot sauce

1. Turn the Instant Pot on to [Sauté]. Heat 1 tablespoon (15 ml) of the olive oil. Add half the kielbasa and cook, turning once, until browned, 3 to 4 minutes. Transfer to a plate. Repeat with the remaining 1 tablespoon (15 ml) olive oil and kielbasa.

2. Add the onion and cook, stirring occasionally, for 3 minutes. Stir in the garlic and cook for 1 minute.

3. Add the black-eyed peas, broth, jalapeño, and kielbasa. Press [Cancel].

4. Lock the lid. Press [Manual] and cook on high pressure for 12 minutes. Use the "Natural Release" method for 10 minutes, then vent any remaining steam and open the lid.

5. Fold in the scallions and spinach. Serve over rice with hot sauce.

Instant Pot

Sticky and Sweet Sriracha Ribs

YIELD:
4 to 6 servings
PREP TIME:
15 minutes
COOK TIME:
35 minutes

INGREDIENTS

½ cup (120 ml) white vinegar
¼ cup (60 g) packed dark
   brown sugar,
1 teaspoon chili powder
1 teaspoon paprika (preferably
   smoked)
1 teaspoon ground cumin
1 teaspoon kosher salt
½ teaspoon freshly ground
   black pepper
4 pounds (1.8 kg) baby back ribs,
   cut into individual ribs
3 tablespoons (60 g) apricot jam
1 to 2 tablespoons (15 to 30 ml)
   sriracha hot sauce

1. Insert the steam rack into the Instant Pot and add the vinegar.

2. In a small bowl, combine the brown sugar, chili powder, paprika, cumin, salt, and pepper to make the rub.

3. Put the ribs into a large bowl, sprinkle with the rub, and toss to coat evenly. Stack the ribs on the steam rack. Lock the lid. Press [Manual] and cook on high pressure for 20 minutes. Use the "Quick Release" method to vent the steam, then open the lid.

4. Line a rimmed baking sheet with aluminum foil and transfer the ribs to it. Remove the steam rack from the Instant Pot.

5. Press [Cancel], then press [Sauté]. Whisk the jam and sriracha into the sauce, and simmer until thickened, about 10 minutes. Skim off and discard as much fat as you can from the sauce.

6. Preheat broiler.

7. Spoon half of the sauce over the ribs. Broil until slightly charred, 2 to 3 minutes. Flip the ribs, spoon over the remaining sauce, and broil 2 to 3 minutes more. Serve immediately.

Instant
Pot

Sauté   Manual

Pozole

YIELD:
4 servings
PREP TIME:
25 minutes
COOK TIME:
1 hour

INGREDIENTS

2 tablespoons (30 ml) extra-
   virgin olive oil
1½ pounds (680 g) boneless pork
   shoulder, trimmed and cut into
   3-inch (7.5 cm) pieces
1½ teaspoons dried oregano
1 teaspoon kosher salt
½ teaspoon freshly ground
   black pepper
4 large cloves garlic, smashed
1 to 2 jalapeños, seeded,
   if desired, and quartered
1 large white onion, chopped
1 pound (454 g) tomatillos, husks
   removed and halved
4 cups (950 ml) less-sodium
   chicken broth
1 bottle (12 ounces, or 355 ml)
   pale lager beer (such as
   Corona)
1 bunch fresh cilantro (including
   stems), divided
1 can (28 ounces, or 795 g)
   hominy, rinsed and drained
¼ cup (60 ml) fresh lime juice

FOR SERVING
Sliced radishes
Diced avocado
Lime wedges

1. Turn the Instant Pot on to [Sauté]. Heat the olive oil. Season
   the pork with the oregano, salt, and pepper, and cook until
   browned, about 6 minutes. Transfer to a plate.

2. Add the garlic, jalapeño, and all but 2 tablespoons of the
   onion, and cook, stirring occasionally, for 3 minutes.

3. Add the tomatillos, chicken broth, beer, and one-third of
   the cilantro. Return the pork to the pot, nesting it in the
   vegetable mixture. Press [Cancel].

4. Lock the lid. Press [Manual] and cook on high pressure for
   45 minutes. Use the "Quick Release" method to vent the
   steam, then open the lid.

5. Remove and discard the cilantro from the pot, and transfer
   the pork to a plate. Add all but ½ cup (8 g) of the remaining
   cilantro and, using a handheld immersion blender (or a
   regular blender), purée the soup.

6. Using 2 forks, break the pork into smaller pieces. Add the
   pork and hominy to the pot. Turn the pot on to [Sauté] and
   cook until the hominy is tender, about 3 minutes. Stir in the
   lime juice.

7. Divide among bowls. Top with radishes, avocado, the reserved
   onion, and the reserved ½ cup (8 g) cilantro (thick stems
   discarded). Serve with lime wedges for squeezing.

Instant
Pot

Sage and Rosemary Pork Loin

YIELD:
4 servings
PREP TIME:
20 minutes
COOK TIME:
35 minutes

INGREDIENTS

4 cloves garlic, finely chopped
12 fresh sage leaves, chopped
1 tablespoon (2 g) chopped fresh rosemary
2 tablespoons (30 ml) extra-virgin olive oil, divided
1½ pounds (680 g) center-cut pork loin
¾ teaspoon kosher salt
½ teaspoon freshly ground black pepper
¼ cup (60 ml) dry white wine, such as Pinot Grigio

1. In a small bowl, combine the garlic, sage, rosemary, and 1 tablespoon (15 ml) of the olive oil.

2. Spacing about 1 inch (2.5 cm) apart, insert the tip of your paring knife 6 times and about 1 inch (2.5 cm) deep into the top of the pork. Fill each opening with some of the herb mixture. Rub the remaining mixture over the pork and season with the salt and pepper.

3. Turn the Instant Pot on to [Sauté]. Heat the remaining 1 tablespoon (15 ml) olive oil. Add the pork and cook until golden brown on all sides, 10 to 12 minutes. Add the wine. Press [Cancel].

4. Lock the lid. Press [Manual] and cook on high pressure for 25 minutes. Use the "Quick Release" method to vent the steam, then open the lid.

5. Transfer the pork to a cutting board and let rest for 5 minutes. Slice the pork and spoon over some of the jus.

Air Fry

YIELD:
4 servings
PREP TIME:
10 minutes
COOK TIME:
35 minutes

Baby Back Ribs

INGREDIENTS

1 rack baby back ribs, membrane removed
1½ teaspoons kosher salt
½ teaspoon freshly ground black pepper
2 teaspoons smoked paprika
1 teaspoon brown sugar
½ teaspoon mustard powder
½ teaspoon garlic powder
¼ cup (60 ml) your favorite barbecue sauce

1. Cut the ribs into 4 pieces. In a small bowl, combine the salt, pepper, smoked paprika, brown sugar, mustard powder, and garlic powder. Rub all over the ribs.

2. Transfer to the Air Fryer rack, rounded-side down, and cook at 360°F (185°C) for 15 minutes. Turn the ribs over and cook for 15 minutes longer.

3. Brush the barbecue sauce on top, increase the heat to 400°F (205°C), and cook for 5 minutes longer.

Air Fry

YIELD:
2 servings
PREP TIME:
10 minutes, plus
10 minutes to rest
COOK TIME:
13 minutes

Pork Katsu

INGREDIENTS

PORK
½ cup (60 g) panko bread crumbs
1 teaspoon water
2 tablespoons (16 g) all-purpose flour
¼ teaspoon kosher salt
1 large egg
Two ½-inch (1.3 cm)-thick boneless pork chops, fat rind removed
Cooking spray

SAUCE
1 tablespoon (15 g) ketchup
2 teaspoons Worcestershire sauce
1 teaspoon oyster sauce
1 teaspoon sugar

Shredded white cabbage, for serving

1. To make the pork: In a large shallow bowl or pie dish, combine the panko and water, mix with your hand, and set aside for 10 minutes.

2. In a second large shallow bowl or pie dish, whisk together the flour and salt.

3. In a third large shallow bowl or pie dish, lightly beat the egg.

4. Use a meat mallet or rolling pin to pound the pork into ½-inch (1.3 cm)-thick pieces. Coat the pork chops in the flour mixture, then coat in the egg, tapping off the excess. Coat in the panko bread crumbs.

5. Spray the pork chops on both sides with the cooking spray and transfer to the Air Fryer rack. Cook at 380°F (195°C) for 8 minutes. Turn and cook until golden brown and crispy, about 5 minutes more.

6. To make the sauce: Meanwhile, in a small bowl, combine the ketchup, Worcestershire sauce, oyster sauce, and sugar. Serve with the pork and shredded white cabbage.

Air Fryer

Sweet and Sour Pork Chops

YIELD:
2 servings
PREP TIME:
10 minutes, plus 2 hours to marinate
COOK TIME:
10 minutes

INGREDIENTS

- 1 tablespoon (15 ml) canola oil
- 1 tablespoon (15 ml) oyster sauce
- 1 tablespoon (15 ml) low-sodium soy sauce
- 1 tablespoon (15 ml) fish sauce
- 1 teaspoon honey
- 1 clove garlic, very finely grated or pressed
- 1-inch (2.5 cm) piece ginger, peeled and very finely grated
- Two ¾-inch (2 cm)-thick boneless pork chops, fat rind removed
- ½ cup (85 g) raw rice
- ½ cup (8 g) roughly chopped fresh cilantro leaves
- 1 scallion, thinly sliced

1. In a large zip-top bag, combine the oil, oyster sauce, soy sauce, fish sauce, honey, garlic, and ginger. Massage the bag to mix together, then add the pork chops and massage to coat. Seal the bag and refrigerate for at least 2 hours or up to 24 hours.

2. Cook the rice according to the package directions.

3. While the rice is cooking, transfer the pork chops to the Air Fryer rack and cook at 380°F (195°C) for 8 minutes. Flip and continue cooking for 2 minutes longer or to your desired doneness.

4. Toss cooked rice with cilantro and divide it amongst two bowls. Plate the pork chops over the rice, sprinkling with scallions to serve.

Air
Fryer

Chorizo and Mushroom Empanadas

Air Fry

YIELD:
8 empanadas
PREP TIME:
8 minutes
COOK TIME:
15 minutes

INGREDIENTS

- 1 tablespoon (15 ml) extra-virgin olive oil
- 1 small onion, finely chopped
- 4 ounces (112 g) mushrooms, roughly chopped
- 6 ounces (168 g) fresh chorizo, skins removed
- 8 empanada wrappers, thawed if frozen
- ¼ cup (38 g) crumbled queso fresco or goat cheese

1. Heat the oil in a large nonstick skillet over medium heat. Add the onion, mushrooms, and chorizo and cook, stirring and breaking up the chorizo with the back of a spoon, until brown and cooked through, 3 to 4 minutes. Transfer to a bowl and let cool to room temperature.

2. Working one at a time, place a wrapper on a clean surface. Place a rounded tablespoon (15 g) of the chorizo mixture and a little cheese in the center. Brush the outer edge of the wrapper lightly with water, then fold over the sides to meet each other and pinch together tightly to seal.

3. Transfer the empanadas to the Air Fryer rack and cook at 380°F (195°C) for 8 minutes, then flip and cook until deep golden brown, 2 to 3 minutes longer.

SEAFOOD MAINS

Instant Pot

Jambalaya

YIELD:
4 servings
PREP TIME:
20 minutes
COOK TIME:
25 minutes

INGREDIENTS

1 tablespoon (15 ml) extra-virgin olive oil
2 ribs celery, thinly sliced
1 medium yellow onion, finely chopped
1 green bell pepper, seeded and cut into ½-inch (13 mm) pieces
2 cloves garlic, finely chopped
6 ounces (170 g) andouille sausage, cut into ¼-inch-thick (6 mm) pieces
1 can (14½ ounces, or 410 g) diced tomatoes
¾ teaspoon kosher salt
½ teaspoon dried oregano
½ teaspoon dried thyme
¼ teaspoon cayenne pepper
¼ teaspoon freshly ground black pepper
1 bay leaf
1 cup (195 g) long-grain white rice
1 cup (235 ml) water
8 ounces (225 g) medium shrimp, peeled and deveined
¼ cup (15 g) chopped fresh flat-leaf parsley
2 scallions (white and light green parts), thinly sliced

1. Turn the Instant Pot on to [Sauté]. Heat the olive oil. Add the celery, onion, and bell pepper, and cook, stirring occasionally, until softened, 5 to 6 minutes.

2. Add the garlic and sausage and cook, stirring, for 1 minute. Add the tomatoes, salt, oregano, thyme, cayenne, black pepper, bay leaf, rice, and water, and stir to combine. Press [Cancel].

3. Lock the lid. Press [Manual] and cook on high pressure for 8 minutes. Use the "Quick Release" method to vent the steam, then open the lid. Stir in the shrimp. Lock the lid and let stand for 10 minutes.

4. Discard the bay leaf and stir in the parsley, then sprinkle with the scallions.

Instant Pot

Manhattan Clam Chowder

YIELD:
4 servings
PREP TIME:
20 minutes
COOK TIME:
15 minutes

INGREDIENTS

4 slices bacon, chopped
1 yellow onion, chopped
2 cloves garlic, finely chopped
2 ribs celery, cut into ¼-inch
   (6 mm) pieces
2 medium carrots, cut into
   ¼-inch (6 mm) pieces
1 green bell pepper, seeded and
   cut into ¼-inch (6 mm) pieces
2 cans (6 ounces, or 170 g)
   chopped clams
2 bottles (8 ounces, or 235 ml,
   each) clam juice
1 can (28 ounces, or 795 g)
   whole peeled tomatoes
2 medium Yukon gold potatoes
   (about 12 ounces, or 340 g),
   cut into ½-inch (13 mm) pieces
6 sprigs fresh thyme
2 bay leaves
¼ teaspoon crushed red
   pepper flakes
2 tablespoons (8 g) chopped
   fresh flat-leaf parsley
Crusty bread, for serving

1. Turn the Instant Pot on to [Sauté]. Add the bacon and cook, stirring, for 4 minutes. Add the onion and cook, stirring occasionally, until beginning to soften, about 3 minutes. Stir in the garlic and cook for 1 minute. Stir in the celery, carrots, and the bell pepper.

2. Open the cans of clams and drain the juice into a large measuring cup. Set the clams aside. Add enough water to equal 2 cups (475 ml).

3. Add the clam juice–water mixture and the bottles of clam juice to the pot and cook, stirring and scraping up any brown bits, for 1 minute. Add the tomatoes (and their juices) to the pot, crushing them with your hands as you add them. Add the potatoes, thyme, bay leaves, and red pepper flakes. Press [Cancel].

4. Lock the lid. Press [Manual] and cook on high pressure for 4 minutes. Use the "Quick Release" method to vent the steam, then open the pot.

5. Discard the thyme and bay leaves. Stir in the clams and cook until heated through, about 2 minutes. Stir in the parsley and serve immediately with crusty bread.

Instant Pot

Sauté   Manual

Italian-Style Seafood Stew

YIELD:
4 to 6 servings
PREP TIME:
20 minutes
COOK TIME:
10 minutes

INGREDIENTS

2 tablespoons (30 ml) extra-virgin olive oil

2 ribs celery, sliced

1 leek (white and light green parts only), sliced into ¼-inch-thick (6 mm) half-moons

1 small bulb fennel, quartered, cored, and sliced

2 large cloves garlic, thinly sliced

2 tablespoons (32 g) tomato paste

1 cup (235 ml) dry white wine, such as Pinot Grigio

1½ pounds (680 g) plum tomatoes, chopped

1 pound (454 g) cod, cut into 2-inch (5 cm) pieces

8 ounces (225 g) large shrimp, peeled and deveined

1 pound (454 g) mussels

1 tablespoon (15 ml) sherry vinegar

Crusty bread, for serving

Chopped fresh flat-leaf parsley, for serving

1. Turn the Instant Pot on to [Sauté]. Heat the olive oil. Add the celery, leek, and fennel, and cook, stirring occasionally, for 2 minutes. Add the garlic and cook, stirring, for 1 minute. Add the tomato paste and cook, stirring, for 1 minute.

2. Add the wine and tomatoes and toss to combine. Press [Cancel]. Place the cod on top of the vegetables. Press [Manual] and cook on low pressure for 2 minutes. Use the "Quick Release" method to vent the steam, then open the lid.

3. Press [Cancel], then press [Sauté]. Nestle the shrimp in the mixture and cook for 2 minutes. Add the mussels, cover the pot, and cook until the shrimp are opaque throughout and the mussels have opened, about 3 minutes. Press [Cancel], open the lid, and stir in the vinegar.

4. Serve with crusty bread and a sprinkle of parsley.

Instant Pot

Sauté · Manual

Cod Cakes in a Tangy Tomato Sauce

YIELD:
4 servings
PREP TIME:
25 minutes
COOK TIME:
20 minutes

INGREDIENTS

COD CAKES
1 pound (454 g) cod, chopped into small pieces
⅓ cup (38 g) dried bread crumbs
2 scallions (white and light green parts), finely chopped
2 tablespoons (8 g) chopped fresh flat-leaf parsley, plus more for serving
2 tablespoons (2 g) chopped fresh cilantro
1 teaspoon finely grated orange zest
½ teaspoon ground cumin
½ teaspoon kosher salt
¼ teaspoon freshly ground black pepper
2 large eggs, beaten
2 tablespoons (30 ml) extra-virgin olive oil, plus more if necessary

SAUCE
1 can (14½ ounces, or 410 g) crushed tomatoes
1 clove garlic, finely chopped
1 teaspoon paprika
1 teaspoon sugar
½ teaspoon kosher salt
¼ teaspoon black pepper
¼ teaspoon crushed red pepper flakes

1. To make the cod cakes, in a large bowl, combine the cod, bread crumbs, scallions, parsley, cilantro, orange zest, cumin, salt, and pepper. Add the eggs and gently mix in until well combined. Shape into 8 patties about 1 inch (2.5 cm) thick. Refrigerate for 5 minutes.

2. To make the sauce, in a medium bowl, combine the tomatoes, garlic, paprika, sugar, salt, black pepper, and red pepper flakes.

3. Turn the Instant Pot on to [Sauté]. Heat the olive oil. Add 4 of the cod cakes and cook until golden brown, 2 to 3 minutes per side. Transfer to a plate. Repeat with the remaining cod cakes, adding more olive oil to the pot if necessary.

4. Add the sauce to the pot. Press [Cancel]. In a single layer, nestle the cod cakes in the sauce. Lock the lid. Press [Manual] and cook on low pressure for 8 minutes. Use the "Quick Release" method to vent the steam, then open the lid.

5. Divide the cod cakes and sauce among plates and sprinkle with parsley.

Instant Pot

Salmon with Soy-Ginger Butter and Bok Choy

YIELD:
4 servings
PREP TIME:
10 minutes
COOK TIME:
10 minutes

INGREDIENTS

- 1 tablespoon (8 g) sesame seeds
- ¼ cup (½ stick, or 60 g) unsalted butter, at room temperature
- 1 tablespoon (8 g) grated fresh ginger
- 2 scallions (white and light green parts), finely chopped
- 1 teaspoon less-sodium soy sauce
- 4 fillets (6 ounces, or 170 g, each) salmon
- 4 baby bok choy, halved lengthwise
- 1 lemon, quartered

1. Turn the Instant Pot on to [Sauté]. Add the sesame seeds and toast, stirring often, until golden brown, 2 to 3 minutes. Press [Cancel]. Transfer to a small bowl.

2. Insert the steam rack into the Instant Pot. Add 1½ cups (350 ml) water.

3. In small bowl, stir together the butter, ginger, scallions, and soy sauce.

4. Tear off a large piece of parchment paper about 20 inches (51 cm) long, and fold it in half. Open it up, place the salmon pieces on one half of the paper, and, dividing evenly, spoon the butter mixture over each piece. Fold the parchment over to cover and make small overlapping folds to seal the edges.

5. Place the parchment packet on the steam rack. Lay the bok choy on top. Lock the lid. Press [Manual] and cook on low pressure for 8 minutes. Use the "Quick Release" method to vent the steam, then open the lid.

6. Divide the bok choy among plates. Lift the packet out and open up. Serve the salmon alongside the bok choy. Top with the sesame seeds and serve with the lemon quarters for squeezing.

Air Fry

Teriyaki Salmon

YIELD:
2 servings
PREP TIME:
15 minutes
COOK TIME:
15 minutes

INGREDIENTS

3 tablespoons (45 ml)
low-sodium soy sauce
1 tablespoon (15 ml) water
1 tablespoon (12 g) brown sugar
½-inch (1.3 cm) piece ginger,
peeled and finely grated
(about 1 teaspoon)
1 clove garlic, finely grated
Two 6-ounce (168 g) salmon fillets

1. Place the soy sauce, water, brown sugar, ginger, and garlic in a small saucepan and gently simmer until the sugar dissolves and the mixture is slightly syrupy, about 2 minutes.

2. Line the Air Fryer rack with parchment paper. Brush the salmon pieces with the sauce and transfer to the prepared rack. Cook at 370°F (190°C) until the fish is opaque throughout, 10 to 15 minutes.

Air Fryer

Coconut Shrimp Tacos

YIELD:
2 servings
PREP TIME:
20 minutes
COOK TIME:
8 minutes

INGREDIENTS

SHRIMP
2 tablespoons (16 g) all-purpose flour
¼ teaspoon freshly ground black pepper
1 large egg
¼ cup (30 g) panko bread crumbs
2 tablespoons (10 g) shredded unsweetened coconut
1 teaspoon melted coconut oil or canola oil
16-20 shrimp, peeled and deveined

SLAW
1 tablespoon (15 g) yogurt
1 tablespoon (15 g) mayonnaise
1 tablespoon (15 ml) fresh lime juice
⅛ teaspoon kosher salt
⅛ teaspoon freshly ground black pepper
8 ounces (227 g) cabbage, finely shredded

4 small flour or corn tortillas, warmed
Sliced avocado, for serving (optional)

1. To make the shrimp: In a large shallow bowl or pie dish, whisk together the flour and pepper. In a second large bowl, lightly beat the egg. In a third large shallow bowl or pie dish, combine the panko, coconut, and melted coconut oil.

2. Working one at a time, coat the shrimp in the flour mixture, then the egg, tapping off the excess, then coat in the coconut mixture. Repeat with the remaining shrimp. Transfer to the Air Fryer rack and cook at 400°F (205°C) until golden brown and the shrimp are opaque throughout, 6 to 8 minutes.

3. To make the slaw: Meanwhile, in a large bowl, whisk together the yogurt, mayonnaise, lime juice, salt, and pepper. Toss in the cabbage and stir to coat. Serve the cabbage with the shrimp inside warm tortillas and top with avocado, if desired.

Cornflake-Crusted Fish Sandwiches with Tartar Sauce

Air Fry

YIELD:
2 servings
PREP TIME:
20 minutes
COOK TIME:
10 minutes

INGREDIENTS

FISH
½ cup (15 g) cornflakes,
   lightly crushed
1 teaspoon extra-virgin olive oil
10 ounces (280 g) skinless cod,
   patted dry, cut into 2 pieces
¼ teaspoon kosher salt
⅛ teaspoon freshly ground
   black pepper
2 teaspoons Dijon mustard

SAUCE
¼ cup (60 g) plain yogurt
2 cornichons, finely chopped
1 tablespoon (4 g) finely
   chopped fresh flat-leaf parsley
1 teaspoon fresh lemon juice
Pinch of kosher salt
Pinch of freshly ground
   black pepper

2 hamburger buns, warmed and
   split open

1. To make the fish: In a small bowl, combine the cornflakes and olive oil. Season the fish with the salt and pepper and brush with the mustard. Press the cornflakes on top of the mustard, then transfer the fish to the Air Fryer rack. Cook at 380°F (195°C) until the fish is opaque throughout, 8 to 10 minutes.

2. To make the sauce: Meanwhile, in a small bowl, combine the yogurt, cornichons, parsley, lemon juice, salt, and pepper. Serve the fish in the buns, topped with the tartar sauce.

Air Fryer

Crab Cakes

YIELD:
8 crab cakes

PREP TIME:
15 minutes, plus 1 hour minimum to chill

COOK TIME:
16 minutes

INGREDIENTS

2 tablespoons (30 g) mayonnaise
1 tablespoon (15 ml) fresh lemon juice
1 teaspoon finely grated lemon zest
2 scallions, finely chopped
¼ cup (16 g) roughly chopped fresh flat-leaf parsley
2 teaspoons Dijon mustard
1 large egg, beaten
½ teaspoon paprika
¼ teaspoon kosher salt
⅛ teaspoon freshly ground black pepper
1 pound (454 g) lump crabmeat, picked over for shells
½ cup (60 g) bread crumbs

1. In a large bowl, combine the mayonnaise, lemon juice, lemon zest, scallions, parsley, mustard, egg, paprika, salt, and pepper. Fold in the crab and bread crumbs. Form the mixture into 8 rounded balls (about ½ cup, or 120 g, each). Refrigerate for at least 1 hour or up to 24 hours.

2. Line an Air Fryer rack with parchment paper. Transfer half of the crab cakes to the prepared rack. Cook at 400°F (205°C) until golden, 8 minutes. Repeat with the remaining crab cakes.

VEGETABLE MAINS

Instant Pot

Manual

Layered Vegetable Casserole

YIELD:
4 servings
PREP TIME:
20 minutes
COOK TIME:
40 minutes

INGREDIENTS

- 2 tablespoons (30 ml) extra-virgin olive oil, divided, plus more for soufflé dish
- 1 can (15 ounces, or 425 g) cannellini beans, rinsed and drained
- 1 clove garlic, peeled
- ¼ cup (25 g) grated Parmesan cheese, plus more for sprinkling
- ½ teaspoon kosher salt, divided
- 1 sweet potato (about 10 ounces, or 280 g), peeled
- 1 Yukon gold potato (about 8 ounces, or 225 g), unpeeled
- 1 rutabaga (about 8 ounces, or 225 g), peeled
- 2 red beets (each about 5 ounces, or 140 g), peeled
- 1 teaspoon fresh thyme leaves
- 2 tablespoons (8 g) chopped fresh flat-leaf parsley
- ⅛ teaspoon freshly ground black pepper

1. Insert the steam rack into the Instant Pot. Add 1½ cups (350 ml) water. Oil a deep 8-inch (20 cm) round soufflé or casserole dish.

2. In a food processor, purée the beans, garlic, Parmesan, 1 tablespoon (15 ml) of the olive oil, and ¼ teaspoon of the salt until smooth. Spread the purée evenly into the bottom of the dish.

3. Using a chef's knife or mandoline, slice the sweet potato, Yukon gold potato, rutabaga, and beets into about ⅛-inch-thick (3 mm) slices.

4. Arrange the vegetables upright, fitting them snugly together in a pinwheel fashion, alternating as you go. Drizzle with the remaining 1 tablespoon (15 ml) olive oil. Sprinkle with the thyme and the remaining ¼ teaspoon salt.

5. Using aluminum foil, make a "sling" measuring about 3 x 20 inches (7.5 x 51 cm). Use it to lower the dish into the pot. Lock the lid. Press [Manual] and cook on high pressure for 25 minutes. Use the "Natural Release" method for 15 minutes, then vent any remaining steam and open the lid.

6. Sprinkle the casserole with a little more Parmesan and the parsley and pepper.

Instant Pot

Manual

Vegetable Green Thai Curry

YIELD:
4 servings
PREP TIME:
15 minutes
COOK TIME:
6 minutes

INGREDIENTS

1 can (13½ ounces, or 400 ml) coconut milk

½ cup (120 ml) water

¾ teaspoon kosher salt

1 medium eggplant (about 1 pound, or 454 g), cut into ¾-inch (2 cm) pieces

1 large sweet potato (about 1 pound, or 454 g), cut into ¾-inch (2 cm) pieces

1 pint grape tomatoes (25 to 30 tomatoes)

1 jalapeño, seeded

1 piece (1 inch, or 2.5 cm) fresh ginger, peeled and sliced

1 clove garlic, peeled

2 cups (32 g) fresh cilantro leaves

3 tablespoons (45 ml) extra-virgin olive oil

Jasmine rice, for serving

1. To the Instant Pot, add the coconut milk, water, and salt. Add the eggplant, sweet potato, and tomatoes. Lock the lid. Press [Manual] and cook on high pressure for 6 minutes. Use the "Quick Release" method to release the steam, then open the lid.

2. In a food processor, purée the jalapeño, ginger, garlic, cilantro, and oil until smooth. Stir into the vegetables.

3. Serve the curry over jasmine rice.

Instant Pot

Artichokes Stuffed with Parmesan Bread Crumbs

YIELD:
4 servings
PREP TIME:
20 minutes
COOK TIME:
20 minutes

INGREDIENTS

4 medium globe artichokes
1 cup (100 g) grated Parmesan cheese
¾ cup (90 g) dried bread crumbs
½ cup (30 g) chopped fresh flat-leaf parsley
¼ cup (24 g) chopped fresh mint
2 cloves garlic, finely chopped
¾ teaspoon kosher salt
¼ teaspoon freshly ground black pepper
½ cup (120 ml) extra-virgin olive oil, plus more for drizzling
1 pint grape tomatoes (25 to 30 tomatoes), cut into small pieces

1. Insert the steam rack into the Instant Pot. Add 1½ cups (350 ml) water.

2. Trim the top quarter from the artichokes and discard. Trim and reserve the stems so the artichokes sit flat. Place the artichokes and stems in the steam rack and lock the lid. Press [Manual] and cook on high pressure for 20 minutes. Use the "Quick Release" method to vent the steam, then open the lid. Let cool to room temperature.

3. Gently spread apart the leaves of the artichokes. Use a melon baller to scoop out and discard the chokes. Chop the stems.

4. In a medium bowl, combine the chopped stems, Parmesan, bread crumbs, parsley, mint, garlic, salt, and pepper. Stir in the olive oil, then fold in the tomatoes.

5. Fill the center of each artichoke with bread crumb mixture, then spoon the remaining mixture in between the leaves. Drizzle a little more oil over the top, and serve.

Instant Pot

Minestrone Soup

YIELD:
6 servings
PREP TIME:
15 minutes
COOK TIME:
15 minutes

INGREDIENTS

- 1 tablespoon (15 ml) extra-virgin olive oil
- 1 medium yellow onion, finely chopped
- 2 cloves garlic, finely chopped
- 2 tablespoons (32 g) tomato paste
- 2 containers (32 ounces, or 950 ml, each) less-sodium vegetable broth
- 2 medium carrots, sliced into half-moons
- 2 ribs celery, sliced
- 2 medium red potatoes (about 8 ounces, or 225 g), cut into 1-inch (2.5 cm) pieces
- ¼ small head Savoy cabbage, cored and cut into 1-inch (2.5 cm) pieces
- 1 cup (93 g) ditalini or other small pasta
- ½ teaspoon kosher salt
- ½ teaspoon freshly ground black pepper
- 1 can (15 ounces, or 425 g) kidney beans, rinsed and drained
- 1 cup (130 g) frozen peas, thawed
- 1 bunch spinach, thick stems discarded
- Grated Parmesan cheese, for serving
- Prepared pesto, for serving

1. Turn the Instant Pot on to [Sauté]. Heat the olive oil. Add the onion and cook, stirring occasionally, for 3 minutes. Add the garlic and cook, stirring, for 1 minute. Add the tomato paste and cook, stirring, for 1 minute.

2. Add the vegetable broth and cook, stirring and scraping up any brown bits, for 1 minute. Add the carrots, celery, potatoes, cabbage, pasta, salt, and pepper. Press [Cancel].

3. Lock the lid. Press [Manual] and cook on high pressure for 3 minutes. Use the "Quick Release" method to vent the steam, then open the lid.

4. Add the beans and peas, and cook until heated through, about 2 minutes. Add the spinach and cook until beginning to wilt, about 1 minute.

5. Ladle into bowls and serve with Parmesan and a dollop of pesto.

Instant Pot

Spinach and Herb Lasagna

YIELD:
4 to 6 servings
PREP TIME:
20 minutes
COOK TIME
25 minutes

INGREDIENTS

1 large egg
½ teaspoon kosher salt
½ teaspoon freshly ground black pepper
1 pound (454 g) ricotta cheese
¼ cup (25 g) grated Pecorino cheese
8 ounces (225 g) fresh mozzarella cheese, coarsely shredded
2 cups (60 g) baby spinach, chopped
¼ cup (15 g) chopped fresh flat-leaf parsley
¼ cup (10 g) chopped fresh basil
2½ cups (595 ml) your favorite marinara sauce
8 no-boil lasagna noodles

1. Insert the steam rack into the Instant Pot and add 1½ cups (350 ml) water. In a medium bowl, beat the egg with the salt and pepper. Add the ricotta, Pecorino, and ½ cup (60 g) of the mozzarella, and mix to combine. Fold in the spinach, parsley, and basil.

2. Spread ½ cup (120 ml) of the marinara on the bottom of a deep 8-inch (20 cm) round soufflé or casserole dish. Top with 2 noodles, breaking them to fit as necessary, then spread ½ cup (120 ml) of the marinara over the top. Dollop with one-third of the ricotta mixture and sprinkle with one-quarter of the remaining mozzarella.

3. Top with 2 noodles, breaking them to fit as necessary, and spread ½ cup (120 ml) of the marinara and another one-third each of the ricotta mixture and the mozzarella. Repeat once more. Finish by topping with the remaining 2 noodles, ½ cup (120 g) of sauce, and a quarter of mozzarella.

4. Cover the dish with aluminum foil. Using another piece of foil, make a "sling" measuring about 3 x 20 inches (7.5 x 51 cm). Use it to lower the pan into the pot.

5. Lock the lid. Press [Manual] and cook on high pressure for 10 minutes. Use the "Natural Release" method for 15 minutes, then vent any remaining steam and open the lid. Lift the lasagna from the pot and discard the foil.

6. If desired, preheat broiler and broil the lasagna until the cheese is golden brown, 2 to 3 minutes.

Instant Pot

Broccoli and Parmesan Farrotto

YIELD:
4 servings
PREP TIME:
20 minutes
COOK TIME:
25 minutes

INGREDIENTS

- 2 tablespoons (30 ml) extra-virgin olive oil
- 1 medium yellow onion, finely chopped
- ½ teaspoon kosher salt, divided
- ½ teaspoon freshly ground black pepper, divided, plus more for serving
- 2 cloves garlic, finely chopped
- 1 cup (208 g) farro
- ½ cup (120 ml) dry white wine, such as Pinot Grigio
- 3 cups (700 ml) less-sodium vegetable broth or water
- 1 small bunch broccoli, cut into small florets
- ½ cup (50 g) grated Parmesan cheese, plus more for serving

1. Turn the Instant Pot on to [Sauté]. Heat the olive oil. Add the onion, ¼ teaspoon of the salt, and ¼ teaspoon of the pepper, and cook, stirring occasionally, for 3 minutes. Add the garlic and continue to cook, stirring, for 1 minute. Add the farro and stir to coat in the oil.

2. Add the wine and simmer until it has nearly evaporated, 2 to 3 minutes. Add the broth and press [Cancel]. Lock the lid. Press [Manual] and cook on high pressure for 10 minutes. Use the "Quick Release" method to vent the steam, then open the lid.

3. Press [Cancel], then press [Sauté]. Once the mixture is simmering, add the broccoli and mix to combine. Cover and cook for 3 minutes. Uncover and simmer until the broccoli is tender, about 2 minutes more. Press [Cancel].

4. In 2 additions, fold in the Parmesan, then season with the remaining ¼ teaspoon salt and ¼ teaspoon pepper. Serve sprinkled with a little more Parmesan.

Instant Pot

Baked Sweet Potatoes with Green Apple Slaw

YIELD:
4 servings

PREP TIME:
15 minutes

COOK TIME:
35 minutes

INGREDIENTS

- 4 sweet potatoes (about 12 ounces, or 340 g, each)
- 1 medium fennel bulb, thinly sliced
- 1 green apple, such as Granny Smith, cut into 1-inch (2.5 cm) sticks
- 3 tablespoons (45 ml) fresh lemon juice
- 3 tablespoons (45 ml) extra-virgin olive oil
- ¼ cup (15 g) chopped fresh flat-leaf parsley
- 2 scallions (white and light green parts), thinly sliced
- ¼ cup (37 g) roasted almonds
- ¼ teaspoon kosher salt
- ⅛ teaspoon freshly ground black pepper

1. Insert the steam rack into the Instant Pot. Add 1½ cups (350 ml) water.

2. Pierce the potatoes several times with a fork, then place on the steam rack. Lock the lid. Press [Manual] and cook on high pressure for 20 minutes. Use the "Natural Release" method for 15 minutes, then vent any remaining steam and open the lid.

3. In a medium bowl, combine the fennel, apple, lemon juice, olive oil, parsley, scallions, almonds, salt, and pepper for the slaw.

4. Make a slit in the top of each potato and gently squeeze to open each one up. Spoon the slaw over the potatoes.

Instant Pot

Manual · Sauté

Cheesy Pasta and Kale

YIELD:
4 servings
PREP TIME:
10 minutes
COOK TIME:
15 minutes

INGREDIENTS

12 ounces (340 g) mezze rigatoni
½ cup (120 g) mascarpone cheese, at room temperature
1 tablespoon (11 g) Dijon mustard
⅛ teaspoon freshly grated nutmeg
1½ cups (180 g) grated Gruyère cheese
¼ cup (25 g) grated Parmesan cheese
3 cups (200 g) baby kale
½ teaspoon freshly ground black pepper
¼ teaspoon kosher salt

1. Put the pasta and 4 cups (950 ml) water in the Instant Pot. Lock the lid. Press [Manual] and cook on high pressure for 5 minutes. Use the "Natural Release" method for 5 minutes, then vent any remaining steam and open the lid. Press [Cancel].

2. Reserve ½ cup (120 ml) of the pasta water, then drain the pasta and return it to the pot. Press [Sauté]. Add the mascarpone, mustard, and nutmeg, and toss until the pasta is evenly coated.

3. Add the Gruyère and Parmesan, and toss until the cheeses melt. Stir in some of the reserved pasta water if the sauce is too thick.

4. Add the kale and cook, tossing until just wilted, for about 2 minutes. Season with the pepper and salt. Press [Cancel] and serve immediately.

Air Fryer

Dumplings with Nuoc Cham

YIELD:
40
PREP TIME:
25 minutes
COOK TIME:
35 minutes

INGREDIENTS

DUMPLINGS

4 ounces mushrooms, finely chopped (shitake or button)
2 teaspoons coconut oil or canola oil
1 small leek, finely chopped
4 ounces (about 2) carrots, peeled and coarsely grated
4 ounces broccoli crowns, finely chopped
10 ounces (about ¼ medium) cabbage, cored and shredded
2 garlic cloves, finely grated
1 tablespoon finely grated ginger
2 tablespoons soy sauce
1 tablespoon rice vinegar
1 teaspoon sambal olek
40 dumpling wrappers
Cooking spray

NUOC CHAM SAUCE

⅓ cup (80 ml) fresh lime juice
¼ cup (60 ml) water
1 tablespoon (12 g) sugar
1 tablespoon (15 ml) fish sauce
1 large clove garlic, pressed through a garlic press
1 Thai red chile, thinly sliced

1. To make the dumplings: Heat a large nonstick skillet or wok over medium-high heat. Add the mushrooms and dry-fry, tossing occasionally, until they start to turn golden, around 2 to 3 minutes.

2. Reduce the heat to medium and add the oil, leek and broccoli. Cook for 3 minutes to slightly soften, about 4 minutes.

3. Add the carrot and cabbage and cook, stirring occasionally, 5 to 7 minutes. Then stir in the garlic and ginger. Cook for 1 minute. Remove the pan from the heat and add the soy sauce, vinegar, and sambal olek, stirring to incorporate. Set aside to cool to room temperature.

4. To make the sauce: Meanwhile, in a small bowl or measuring pitcher, combine the lime juice, water, sugar, fish sauce, garlic, and chile, stirring until the sugar dissolves. Serve with the dumplings for dipping.

5. To assemble the dumplings: Working with a few at a time, lay the dumping wrappers flat on a clean work surface. Place a rounded teaspoon of the vegetable mixture in the center. Lightly brush the outside rim of the dumpling wrap with water, then fold in half, pressing together the two sides of the wrapper to seal. Spray each dumpling evenly with cooking spray as you transfer some of the dumplings to the Air Fryer rack in an even layer. Avoid having the edges overlap too much.

6. Air-fry at 370°F (150°C) until golden and crisp, 5 to 7 minutes. Transfer them to a cooling rack and repeat with the remaining dumplings. Un-fried dumplings can be frozen on a sheet pan, then transferred to an airtight container and frozen for up to 3 months. Serve dumplings hot with homemade sauce and enjoy.

Air Fryer

Vegetable-Fried Rice

Air Fry

YIELD:
2 servings
PREP TIME:
15 minutes
COOK TIME:
18 minutes

INGREDIENTS

2 cups (330 g) cooked rice
1 tablespoon (15 ml) water
1 teaspoon vegetable oil
1 teaspoon sesame oil
1 large egg, lightly beaten
½ cup (75 g) peas, thawed
  if frozen
½ cup (75 g) edamame, thawed
  if frozen
1 tablespoon (15 ml) low-sodium
  soy sauce
1 teaspoon fish sauce
½ teaspoon honey
¼ cup (4 g) chopped fresh
  cilantro

1. In a medium bowl, combine the rice, water, vegetable oil, and sesame oil. Transfer to a 6- to 8-inch (15 to 20 cm) aluminum pan and place on the Air Fryer rack. Cook at 350°F (180°C) for 12 minutes.

2. Fold in the egg and cook for 4 minutes longer. Fold in the peas and edamame and cook for 2 minutes more.

3. Transfer to a bowl and toss with the soy sauce, fish sauce, honey, and cilantro.

Air Fry

YIELD:
16 mini falafels
PREP TIME:
20 minutes
COOK TIME:
8 minutes

Falafel

INGREDIENTS

2 scallions, roughly chopped
1 shallot, roughly chopped
¼ cup (4 g) roughly chopped
  fresh cilantro
¼ cup roughly chopped fresh
  flat-leaf parsley
1 clove garlic, roughly chopped
1 can (15 ounces, or 420 g)
  chickpeas, drained and rinsed
1 tablespoon (8 g) all-purpose
  flour
1 teaspoon ground cumin
¼ teaspoon kosher salt
⅛ teaspoon cayenne pepper
Cooking spray
Hummus, tabbouleh, and
  warmed pita bread, for serving

1. Place the scallions, shallot, cilantro, parsley, and garlic in a food processor and pulse to finely chop.

2. Add the chickpeas, flour, cumin, salt, and cayenne pepper and pulse until the mixture holds together when squeezed.

3. Form the mixture into 16 balls and flatten slightly. Spray both sides with cooking spray and transfer to the Air Fryer rack. Cook at 400°F (205°C) until crispy and golden brown, about 8 minutes, turning halfway through cooking. Serve with hummus, tabbouleh, and warmed pita bread.

Toasted Ravioli with Marinara Sauce

YIELD:
2 servings
PREP TIME:
15 minutes
COOK TIME:
16 minutes

INGREDIENTS

1 large egg
¾ cup (90 g) bread crumbs
¼ cup (25 g) grated Parmesan
½ teaspoon dried oregano
1 teaspoon extra-virgin olive oil
8 ounces (227 g) mini frozen ravioli
½ cup (120 ml) marinara sauce, warmed, for serving

1. In a large shallow bowl or pie dish, lightly beat the egg. In a second large shallow bowl or pie dish, combine the bread crumbs, Parmesan, oregano, and olive oil.

2. While the ravioli are still frozen, working with a few at a time, coat completely in the egg and then in the bread crumb mixture. Transfer half of the ravioli to the Air Fryer rack and cook at 390°F (200°C) until golden and crispy, 7 to 8 minutes.

3. Repeat with the remaining ravioli, then serve with the marinara sauce.

Air Fryer

Crispy Tofu Salad

YIELD:
2 servings
PREP TIME:
25 minutes
COOK TIME:
25 minutes

INGREDIENTS

TOFU
1 package (14 ounces, or 392 g) extra-firm tofu
¼ cup (30 g) cornstarch
½ teaspoon garlic powder
½ teaspoon kosher salt
Cooking spray

DRESSING
3 tablespoons (45 ml) low-sodium soy sauce
2 tablespoons (30 ml) fresh lime juice
2 tablespoons (25 g) brown sugar
1 tablespoon (15 ml) extra-virgin olive oil
1 clove garlic, very finely grated
1 inch (2.5 cm) piece ginger, peeled and very finely grated (about 2 teaspoons)
2 scallions, finely chopped

SALAD
8 ounces (227 g) sugar snap peas, trimmed and sliced on the diagonal
1 red bell pepper, cored, seeded, and thinly sliced into 1-inch (2.5 cm)-long pieces
½ English cucumber, chopped
½ cup (8 g) fresh cilantro leaves
1 teaspoon toasted sesame seeds

1. To make the tofu: Slice the tofu into 1-inch (2.5 cm)-thick slices. Pat dry, then cut each slice into 1-inch (2.5 cm)-cubes. In a large zip-top bag, combine the cornstarch, garlic powder, and salt. Add the tofu, seal the bag, and toss to coat evenly.

2. Coat each piece evenly with cooking spray and transfer to Air Fryer rack. Cook at 370°F (190°C) for 10 minutes, shake and spray again with cooking spray. Continue cooking until crisp and golden, 10 to 15 minutes more.

3. To make the dressing: Meanwhile, in a large bowl, whisk together the soy sauce, lime juice, brown sugar, oil, garlic, ginger, and scallions.

4. To make the salad: Add the sugar snap peas, pepper, cucumber, cilantro, and crispy tofu to the bowl with the dressing and toss to coat evenly. Divide between two bowls and sprinkle with the sesame seeds.

DESSERTS

Instant Pot

Manual

YIELD:
6 servings
PREP TIME:
20 minutes
COOK TIME:
1 hour (plus 6 hours
refrigeration time)

Double Chocolate Cheesecake

INGREDIENTS

CRUST
Nonstick vegetable oil
  cooking spray
22 chocolate wafer cookies
1 tablespoon (13 g) granulated
  sugar
¼ teaspoon ground cinnamon
¼ cup (½ stick, or 60g),
  unsalted butter, melted

FILLING
1¼ cups (220 g) semisweet
  chocolate chips
2 packages (8 ounces, or 225 g
  each) cream cheese, at room
  temperature
¾ cup (150 g) granulated sugar
3 large eggs
¼ cup (60 g) sour cream
1 teaspoon pure vanilla extract

WHIPPED CREAM
¾ cup (175 ml) heavy cream
3 tablespoons (23 g)
  confectioners' sugar

TOPPING
A small hunk of chocolate,
  for shaving

1. Insert the steam rack into the Instant Pot. Add 1½ cups (350 ml) water.

2. To make the crust, coat a 7-inch (18 cm) springform pan with cooking spray. Use a food processor or a resealable plastic bag and a rolling pin to grind the cookies. Mix in the sugar, cinnamon, and butter.

3. Using a flat-bottomed glass, press the crumbs evenly on the bottom and 1 inch (2.5 cm) up the sides of the pan. Freeze the crust while you make the filling.

4. To make the filling, in a medium microwave-safe bowl melt the chocolate chips on high, stirring every 30 seconds, until melted and smooth, about 60 seconds total. Let cool to room temperature, keeping the chocolate warm enough to be pourable.

5. In a large bowl, use an electric mixer on medium speed to beat the cream cheese until smooth and creamy. Beat in the sugar until smooth. Add the eggs, one at a time, beating well after each addition and scraping down the sides of the bowl as needed. Beat in the sour cream and vanilla.

6. With the mixer on low speed, pour in the chocolate and mix in completely. Pour the filling into the prepared crust.

7. Tightly wrap the entire pan in aluminum foil. Using another piece of foil, make a "sling" measuring about 3 x 20 inches (7.5 x 51 cm). Use it to lower the pan into the pot.

8. Lock the lid. Press [Manual] and cook on high pressure for 57 minutes. Use the "Quick Release" method to vent the steam, then open the lid.

9. Lift the pan out and remove the foil (the cheesecake will be slightly wobbly in the center). Let cool on a wire cooling rack for 25 minutes, then run a knife around the edges to loosen it from the pan. Refrigerate for at least 6 hours or overnight, until completely set.

10. To make the whipped cream, in a medium bowl, whisk together the cream and confectioners' sugar until soft peaks form.

11. To serve the cheesecake, remove the ring. Spread the whipped cream over the top of the cheesecake, leaving a 1-inch (2.5 cm) border. Use a vegetable peeler to shave the hunk of chocolate over the top.

Instant Pot

Manual

YIELD:
10 servings
PREP TIME:
15 minutes
COOK TIME:
55 minutes

Chocolate-Peanut Butter Brownies

INGREDIENTS

Nonstick vegetable oil
  cooking spray
4 ounces (115 g) bittersweet
  chocolate, chopped
¾ cup (1½ sticks, or 180 g)
  unsalted butter
2 teaspoons instant
  espresso powder
1 teaspoon pure vanilla
  extract
3 large eggs
1 cup (200 g) sugar
1 cup (120 g) all-purpose flour
½ teaspoon kosher salt
¼ teaspoon baking powder
1 cup (175 g) peanut butter chips
½ cup (88 g) bittersweet
  chocolate chips

1. Insert the steam rack into the Instant Pot. Add 1½ cups (350 ml) water. Coat a deep 8-inch (20 cm) round soufflé or casserole dish with cooking spray.

2. In a medium microwave-safe bowl, melt the chocolate and butter on high, stirring every 30 seconds, until melted and smooth, about 60 seconds total. Stir in the espresso powder and vanilla.

3. In a large bowl, beat the eggs and sugar until combined. Add the chocolate mixture and mix to combine. Add the flour, salt, and baking powder, and mix until fully incorporated. Fold in the peanut butter chips and chocolate chips, then scrape the batter into the prepared dish.

4. Cover the dish with aluminum foil. Using another piece of foil, make a "sling" measuring about 3 x 20 inches (7.5 x 51 cm). Use it to lower the dish into the pot.

5. Lock the lid. Press [Manual] and cook on high pressure for 45 minutes. Use the "Natural Release" method for 10 minutes, then vent any remaining steam and open the lid. Transfer the dish to a wire cooling rack, uncover, and let cool for at least 20 minutes before serving.

Instant Pot

Lemon Soufflé Pudding Cake

YIELD:
6 servings
PREP TIME:
10 minutes
COOK TIME:
45 minutes

INGREDIENTS

2 tablespoons (30 g) unsalted butter, melted, plus more for soufflé dish
2 large eggs
¾ cup (150 g) granulated sugar, divided
Grated zest of 2 lemons
⅓ cup (80 ml) fresh lemon juice
¼ cup (30 g) all-purpose flour
⅛ teaspoon kosher salt
1¼ cups (300 ml) whole milk
1 cup (235 ml) heavy cream
¼ cup (30 g) confectioners' sugar, plus more for dusting

1. Insert the steam rack into the Instant Pot. Add 1½ cups (350 ml) water. Butter a deep 8-inch (20 cm) round soufflé or casserole dish.

2. Separate the egg whites and yolks into 2 large bowls.

3. To the egg yolks, whisk in ½ cup (100 g) of the sugar. Add the lemon zest, lemon juice, flour, and salt, and whisk together. Whisk in the milk, then the melted butter.

4. Using an electric mixer, beat the egg whites on medium-high speed until opaque and foamy. With the mixer running, slowly pour in the remaining ¼ cup (50 g) sugar. Beat until shiny, stiff peaks form. Fold one-third of the whites into the lemon mixture. Then gently fold in the remaining whites. Pour the batter into the prepared dish.

5. Cover the dish with aluminum foil, tenting it to allow room for the soufflé to rise. Using another piece of foil, make a "sling" measuring about 3 x 20 inches (7.5 x 51 cm). Use it to lower the dish into the pot.

6. Lock the lid. Press [Manual] and cook on high pressure for 45 minutes. Use the "Quick Release" method to vent the steam, then open the lid. Lift the dish out and uncover.

7. In a medium bowl, whisk together the cream and confectioners' sugar until soft peaks form.

8. Dust the soufflé with confectioners' sugar and serve warm with the whipped cream.

Instant Pot

Manual   Sauté

Sticky Toffee Pudding

YIELD:
6 servings
PREP TIME:
20 minutes
COOK TIME:
35 minutes

INGREDIENTS

PUDDING

- 6 tablespoons (90 g) unsalted butter, melted, plus more for soufflé dish
- 8 dried (but pliable) Medjool dates, pitted
- ¾ cup (180 ml) very hot water
- 1 teaspoon baking soda
- 2 tablespoons (30 ml) dark rum
- ½ cup (100 g) granulated sugar
- 2 large eggs
- 1 cup (120 g) all-purpose flour
- ¼ teaspoon kosher salt

TOFFEE SAUCE

- ¼ cup (½ stick, or 60 g) unsalted butter
- ½ cup (115 g) packed dark brown sugar
- ¼ cup (60 ml) heavy cream
- ½ teaspoon pure vanilla extract
- Pinch of kosher salt

1. Insert the steam rack into the Instant Pot. Add 1½ cups (350 ml) water. Butter a deep 8-inch (20 cm) round soufflé or casserole dish.

2. To make the pudding, in a medium bowl, combine the dates, hot water, baking soda, and rum. Let stand until the dates are very soft, about 15 minutes.

3. In a large bowl, whisk together the sugar and melted butter. Whisk in the eggs, one at a time. Stir in the flour and salt.

4. In a food processor or blender, purée the dates and liquid until smooth. Pour into the batter and stir until incorporated. Pour the batter into the prepared dish.

5. Cover the dish tightly with aluminum foil. Using another piece of foil, make a "sling" measuring about 3 x 20 inches (7.5 x 51 cm). Use it to lower the dish into the pot.

6. Lock the lid. Press [Manual] and cook on high pressure for 30 minutes. Use the "Quick Release" method to vent the steam, then open the lid. Lift the dish out and uncover.

7. To make the toffee sauce, rinse out and dry the inner pot. Press [Sauté]. Add the butter and melt. Add the brown sugar and whisk until melted, about 30 seconds. Whisk in the cream until incorporated and then let simmer, whisking often, for 1 minute. Press [Cancel]. Whisk in the vanilla and salt.

8. Pour the toffee sauce over the pudding and spoon into individual bowls.

Instant Pot

Warm Chocolate Fudge Cakes

YIELD:
6 servings

PREP TIME:
15 minutes

COOK TIME:
20 minutes

INGREDIENTS

Nonstick vegetable oil cooking spray
½ cup (1 stick, or 120 g) unsalted butter
½ cup (100 g) sugar
¼ cup (60 ml) heavy cream
4 ounces (115 g) semisweet chocolate chips
1 teaspoon pure vanilla extract
2 large eggs
2 tablespoons (12 g) unsweetened cocoa powder
1 tablespoon (8 g) all-purpose flour
Pinch of kosher salt
Vanilla ice cream, for serving

1. Insert the steam rack into the Instant Pot. Add 1½ cups (350 ml) water. Coat six 4-ounce (120 ml) heatproof ramekins with cooking spray.

2. In a small saucepan, combine the butter, sugar, and cream over medium heat. Heat the mixture, stirring often, until melted. Add the chocolate chips and vanilla and remove from the heat. Let stand for 1 minute, then whisk until creamy and smooth.

3. In a medium bowl, whisk together the eggs, cocoa powder, flour, and salt. Whisk in the chocolate mixture until incorporated.

4. Dividing evenly, pour the batter into the prepared ramekins. Cover each tightly with aluminum foil. Place in the pot, stacking them as necessary.

5. Lock the lid. Press [Manual] and cook on high pressure for 15 minutes. Use the "Quick Release" method to vent the steam, then open the lid. Lift the ramekins out and uncover.

6. Unmold the cakes and serve warm, topped with ice cream.

Instant Pot

Dulce de Leche Shortbread Cookies

YIELD:
30 sandwich cookies
PREP TIME:
5 minutes
COOK TIME:
45 minutes

INGREDIENTS

1 can (14 ounces, or 425 ml)
    sweetened condensed milk
60 small shortbread cookies

1. Insert the steam rack into the Instant Pot. Pour the condensed milk into a 16-ounce (475 ml) canning jar with a tight-fitting lid. Close the jar. Place the jar on the rack and add enough water to come halfway up the sides of the jar (about 12 cups, or 2.9 L).

2. Lock the lid. Press [Manual] and cook on high pressure for 35 minutes. Use the "Natural Release" method for 10 minutes, then vent any remaining steam and open the lid. Remove the jar from the pot and stir. (This will yield about 1¼ cups, or 350 ml.)

3. Let the dulce de leche cool for 5 minutes, then sandwich between the cookies.

Instant Pot

Crème Brûlée

YIELD:
6 servings
PREP TIME:
15 minutes
COOK TIME:
20 minutes (plus 4 hours refrigeration time)

INGREDIENTS

5 large egg yolks
²⁄₃ cup (130 g) plus 6 tablespoons (75 g) sugar, divided
½ vanilla bean, split lengthwise, or ½ teaspoon pure vanilla extract
2¼ cups (535 ml) heavy cream
¼ cup (60 ml) whole milk

1. Insert the steam rack into the Instant Pot. Add 1½ cups (350 ml) water.

2. In a large bowl, whisk together the egg yolks and ²⁄₃ cup (130 g) of the sugar. Scrape the seeds out of the vanilla bean and whisk into the egg mixture. Whisk in the cream and milk.

3. Pour the custard into six 4-ounce (120 ml) shallow ramekins. Cover each tightly with aluminum foil. Place on the rack, stacking them as necessary.

4. Lock the lid. Press [Manual] and cook on low pressure for 18 minutes. Use the "Quick Release" method to vent the steam, then open the lid. Lift the ramekins out (they will be slightly wobbly in the middle). Let cool on a wire cooling rack for 25 minutes. Refrigerate, covered, for at least 4 hours or overnight, until completely cool and set.

5. To serve, sprinkle the top of each custard with 1 tablespoon (13 g) of the sugar. Use a kitchen blowtorch or the oven broiler to caramelize the sugar until dark golden brown. Serve immediately.

Instant Pot

Pumpkin Spice Cake

YIELD:
8 servings
PREP TIME:
20 minutes
COOK TIME:
50 minutes

INGREDIENTS

CAKE
Nonstick vegetable oil cooking
 spray
1½ cups (180 g) all-purpose flour
1 teaspoon baking powder
½ teaspoon baking soda
½ teaspoon kosher salt
½ teaspoon ground ginger
¼ teaspoon ground cinnamon
⅛ teaspoon ground cloves
⅛ teaspoon ground nutmeg
½ cup (1 stick, or 120 g) unsalted
 butter, at room temperature
½ cup (100 g) granulated sugar
2 large eggs
1 teaspoon pure vanilla extract
¾ cup (184 g) canned pure
 pumpkin
¼ cup (85 g) unsulfured molasses

GLAZE
1 cup (100 g) confectioners'
 sugar
4 teaspoons whole milk, plus
 more if necessary
½ teaspoon pure vanilla extract
1 lemon

1. Insert the steam rack into the Instant Pot. Add 1½ cups (350 ml) water. Coat a 7-inch (18 cm) angel food cake pan with cooking spray.

2. In a medium bowl, whisk together the flour, baking powder, baking soda, salt, ginger, cinnamon, cloves, and nutmeg.

3. Using an electric mixer on medium-high speed, in a large bowl, beat the butter and sugar until light and fluffy, about 3 minutes. Beat in the eggs, one at a time, then the vanilla. Beat in the pumpkin and the molasses. Reduce the mixer speed to low and gradually add the flour mixture, mixing just until incorporated. Scrape the mixture into the prepared pan.

4. Cover the pan with aluminum foil. Using another piece of foil, make a "sling" measuring about 3 x 20 inches (7.5 x 51 cm). Use it to lower the pan into the pot.

5. Lock the lid. Press [Manual] and cook on high pressure for 50 minutes. Use the "Quick Release" method to vent the steam, then open the lid. Transfer the pan to a wire cooling rack, remove the foil, and let cool for 20 minutes before unmolding. Let cool completely.

6. Just before serving, make the glaze. In a small bowl, whisk together the confectioners' sugar, milk, and vanilla extract until smooth and pourable (adding more milk, a few drops at a time, if necessary). Spoon the glaze over the top of the cake and let drizzle down the sides. Using a vegetable peeler, peel the lemon zest in strips. Thinly slice the strips crosswise and sprinkle over the cake.

Air Fryer

Air Fry

YIELD:
8 donuts
PREP TIME:
20 minutes, plus
4½ hours to rise
COOK TIME:
20 minutes

Jelly Donuts

INGREDIENTS

DONUTS
3 large eggs
2¼ cups (270 g) all-purpose flour,
   plus more for dusting
2 tablespoons (25 g) sugar
2 tablespoons (30 ml) milk
1 envelope (¼ ounce, or 7 g)
   active dry yeast
1 teaspoon kosher salt
½ cup (112 g) unsalted
   butter, chilled and cut into
   small pieces

COATING AND FILLING
6 tablespoons (84 g) unsalted
   butter, melted
½ cup (100 g) sugar
½ cup (120 g) jam

1. To make the donuts: Place the eggs, flour, sugar, milk, yeast, and salt in the large bowl of an electric mixer. Beat with the dough hook on low speed until a sticky ball of dough forms.

2. Increase the speed to medium and gradually add the butter (this step should take 5 to 6 minutes). Transfer the dough to a clean bowl, cover, and refrigerate for at least 4 hours or up to 12 hours.

3. On a lightly floured surface, divide the dough into 8 even pieces and roll into balls. Transfer to a large baking sheet and let rise until puffed and nearly doubled in size, about 30 minutes. Carefully transfer 4 donuts to the Air Fryer rack and cook at 350°F (180°C) for 10 minutes. Repeat with the remaining donuts.

4. To make the coating: Meanwhile, melt the butter in a medium saucepan. Place the sugar in a medium bowl. While the donuts are still warm, one at a time, coat each donut in the butter then immediately coat in the sugar. Once cool, slice the donuts in half and fill with jam (1 tablespoon, or 15 g, per donut). If you have a piping bag and nozzle, you have the option to pipe the jam into the donut's center.

Air Fryer

S'mores Bananas

YIELD:
2 servings
PREP TIME:
5 minutes
COOK TIME:
8 minutes

INGREDIENTS

1 medium banana
1 teaspoon sugar
¼ teaspoon ground cinnamon
1 graham cracker, broken into small pieces
1 heaping tablespoon (5 g) mini marshmallows
1 tablespoon (10 g) semisweet chocolate chips

1. Line the Air Fryer rack with parchment paper. Leaving the skin on, slice the banana in half lengthwise.

2. In a small bowl, combine the sugar and cinnamon, then sprinkle evenly over the cut sides of the banana. Transfer to the prepared Air Fryer rack and cook at 400°F (205°C) for 6 minutes.

3. Top with the graham cracker pieces, marshmallows, and chocolate chips. Cook for 2 minutes longer to melt.

Air
Fryer

Air Fry

Chocolate Lava Cakes

YIELD:
4 servings
PREP TIME:
10 minutes
COOK TIME:
9 minutes

INGREDIENTS

Cooking spray
½ cup (112 g) unsalted butter
4 ounces (112 g) bittersweet
  chocolate, chopped
2 large eggs
2 large egg yolks
¼ cup (50 g) sugar
2 teaspoons all-purpose flour

1. Spray four 4-ounce (120 g) ramekins with cooking spray.

2. Melt the butter and chocolate together in the microwave in a microwave-safe bowl, stirring occasionally, until smooth. Set aside and allow to cool slightly.

3. Meanwhile, in a medium bowl using an electric mixer, whisk together the eggs, egg yolks, and sugar until thickened and pale, 3 to 4 minutes.

4. Fold in the melted chocolate mixture and flour. Divide the mixture among the prepared ramekins (rounded ⅓ cup, or 80 g, each). Place on the Air Fryer rack and cook at 370°F (190°C) for 8 to 9 minutes, then serve immediately. The centers will be nice and soft.

Air
Fryer

Caramel Apple Hand Pies

YIELD:
4 pies
PREP TIME:
20 minutes, plus
20 minutes to chill
COOK TIME:
20 minutes

INGREDIENTS

2 tablespoons (28 g) unsalted butter

⅓ cup (65 g) sugar

2 apples (about 12 ounces, or 340 g), peeled and cut into ½-inch (1.3 cm) pieces

Pinch of kosher salt

2 tablespoons (30 ml) heavy cream

All-purpose flour, for dusting

Two 9-inch (23 cm) rolled pie crusts

1. Place the butter, sugar, and apples in a large skillet over medium-high heat and cook, stirring occasionally, until the apples have softened and caramelized, 5 to 7 minutes. Remove from the heat and mix in the salt and cream. Transfer to a bowl and refrigerate until cool to the touch, at least 20 minutes.

2. Meanwhile on a lightly floured work surface, place one pie dough round and lightly roll to make the surface area slightly bigger. Cut the round into quarters, then trim the edges to make 4 rectangles. Discard the scraps or save for another use.

3. Place ¼ cup (60 g) of the apple mixture in the center of 2 of the rectangles. Lightly brush the border with water. Top with the remaining 2 rectangles, pressing gently to seal. Use a fork to crimp the edges and cut a small slit in the center. Repeat with the remaining pie dough and apple mixture. Chill the pies until firm, about 20 minutes.

4. Line the Air Fryer rack with parchment paper. Place 2 of the pies on the rack and cook at 360°F (185°C) for 6 minutes, then rotate and cook until the underside is golden, 2 to 4 minutes more. Repeat with the remaining 2 pies.

Air
Fryer

Air Fry

Lemon & Almond Souffiés

YIELD:
6 servings
PREP TIME:
15 minutes
COOK TIME:
10 minutes

INGREDIENTS

Butter, for greasing
4 large eggs
4 tablespoons (48 g) granulated sugar, divided
1 teaspoon grated lemon zest
3 tablespoons (45 ml) fresh lemon juice
3 tablespoons (24 g) almond flour
¼ teaspoon kosher salt
1 tablespoon (8 g) confectioners' sugar, for dusting

1. Grease six 4-ounce (120 g) ramekins or pudding molds with butter.

2. Separate the eggs, placing 3 egg yolks in one large bowl (reserve the remaining yolk for another use) and place the 4 egg whites in a second, large, very clean bowl.

3. To the egg yolks, add 3 tablespoons (36 g) of the sugar, the lemon zest, lemon juice, almond flour, and salt and whisk to combine.

4. Using an electric mixer, beat the egg whites until foamy. Add the remaining 1 tablespoon (12 g) sugar and continue beating until stiff, glossy peaks form, 2 to 3 minutes. Fold one-third of the egg white mixture into the egg yolk mixture, then fold in the remaining egg whites until just combined. Spoon the mixture into the prepared ramekins (a heaping ½ cup, or 120 g, per ramekin).

5. Transfer to the Air Fryer rack and cook at 360°F (185°C) until puffed and lightly golden, 8 to 10 minutes. Remove from the rack and serve immediately, dusted with confectioners' sugar.

Index